THE
PURPOSE
OF THE
CHURCH
ON EARTH

TONY AZONUCHE

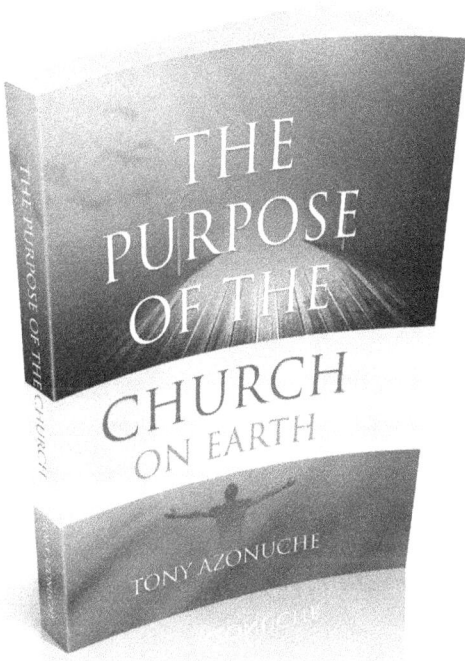

THE PURPOSE OF THE CHURCH ON EARTH

Copyright © 2021 By Tony Azonuche

ISBN: 978-1-64301-029-8

Published in the United States of America by Rehoboth House, Chicago

The opinions expressed by the author in this book are exclusively his and not those of Rehoboth House.

Unless otherwise indicated, all scripture quotations are taken from the Authorized King James Version of the Holy Bible (KJV).

Contact The Author
Tony Azonuche
tonyazonuche@gmail.com
Tel: 1 (832) 419-7961, (832) 419-7988
Convener: Joshua Generation Movement.
Email: joshuagenmovt@gmail.com
For Teachings, Seminars, Workshops on Kingdom Dimensions

Cover And Interior Designed By Rehoboth House, Chicago
rehobothhouseonline.com
info@rehobothhouseonline.com
rehobothpublishing@gmail.com

Printed In United States Of America, December 2021

REHOBOTH HOUSE

CONTENTS

REHOBOTH HOUSE

www.rehobothhouseonline.com

THE PURPOSE OF THE

CHURCH
ON EARTH

DEDICATION

I dedicate this book to all those whose hearts are yearning passionately for the true God and are highly expectant of the manifestation and the revealing of His true Church on earth.

Shalom.

THE PURPOSE OF THE

CHURCH
ON EARTH

ACKNOWLEDGMENT

I am greatly indebted to the Lord Almighty for revelation and insight into the mystery of the dynamics of the Church – the only potentate He has given the authority to govern His entire kingdom. The book 'The Purpose of the Church on Earth' came in as an answer to a groaning prayer request of what I am here on earth for. The Lord not only explained my purpose but equally the purpose of the entire Church. 'The Revealer of all secrets' may your name be praised forever. Amen.

My appreciation goes to my immediate family: my wife, Favor Azonuche, and my children: Wisdom, Davida, Deborah, and Joshua. They have been incredible. They made the writing of this book easy for me. I couldn't have asked for a better family than this. I love you all from my heart.

I want to appreciate all that the Lord has used to shape my thinking process to produce these thoughts. Some I have sat under their ministrations while others I only had the opportunity to read their books or listen to their Online messages. I want to appreciate Rev Bayo Adenugba, Pastor Fola Olumuiyiwa, Pastor Paul Ogedengbe, Dr. Woodfroffe, and the Congress Family, Pastor Taiwo Lemoshe and the GC Family, Apostle Joshua Selman, Pastor Tayo Ladejo, Rev my very own Daddy Falu and Mama Margaret, and the entire River of Life Family; friends and partners of Joshua Generation Movement.

My appreciation goes to friends who have encouraged me in one way or another when the journey sometimes seems very difficult to continue. Bro Isaac Arikawe, Tunde Soetan, Dotun Oluwagbohun, MikePraise Bolum, and host of others. Thank you all for believing in me. You will never lose your reward in Jesus' name.   Amen!

Great thanks to the staff of Rehoboth Publishing House, Chicago, for an impressive work on this book, from editing to finish. What an excellent piece.

ACKNOWLEDGMENT

There are lots of friends, colleagues, and associates whose names are not mentioned here. It does not mean that you are not important, No. My God will reward every one of you beyond my highest prayers in Jesus' name. Amen.

Thank you all.

THE
PURPOSE
OF THE

CHURCH
ON EARTH

CHAPTER 1

PURPOSE AND ITS IMPACT

Purpose can be defined as an anticipated outcome that is intended or that guides your planned actions. It is an intention, aims, or function of something that something is supposed to achieve. It can also be what is needed in a particular situation. Purpose is the reason behind the actions of people and things. It is the force that makes things work. It is possible to have a solid or weak purpose. The complete or partial accomplishment of a purpose determines whether it is strong or weak.

God had a purpose in mind while He was creating the world. He had purposed that His creations will give Him glory, honour, and power. They will declare His works on earth as it is written in **Rev 4:11.**

> *"THOU ART WORTHY, O LORD, to receive glory, honour, and power: for thou hart created all things, and for thy pleasure, they are and were created."*

From this scripture, you find out that the power behind God's motive for creating the world is that they will praise Him. During creation, assuming that some hindrances would have stopped God from going on with creation, once He remembers the purpose, which is to praise Him, He will resist the opposition so He can complete the purpose of creation.

Acts 3:9-11 talks of God's purpose.

> *"...And to make all men see what is the fellowship of the mystery, which from the beginning of the world hath been hid in God, who created all things by Jesus Christ; To the intent that now unto the principalities and powers in heavenly places might be known by the church the manifold wisdom of God, according to the eternal purpose which He purposed in Christ Jesus our Lord."*

In this scripture, you will also find a strong purpose in God. In the final analysis, He had purposed that His Church will show the world, including principalities and powers in the heavenly places, His manifold wisdom. The Church will dazzle the creation about God's wisdom in handling issues and operations. This is His grand plan, so He is ready to wait for it no matter the time it takes the church to get there.

A purpose is powerful, exhilarating, and directional. It sets you on a focus and never leaves you where it met you. It is that which makes you wait for something no matter the time it takes. A thousand years may seem like a year or less in the eyes of a purposeful man. For seven years, Jacob served Laban, his father-in-law, as if it was just a few days because of his love for Rachel. Gen 29:20. Jesus overcame the suffering and humiliations of people and that of the cross because of its purpose, which is the throne of God.

> *"Fixing our eyes on Jesus, the pioneer and perfecter of faith. For the joy set before him, he endured the cross, scorning its shame, and sat down at the right hand of the throne of God" (Heb 12:2).*

The Need For Purpose

As the saying goes, "If purpose is not known, abuse is inevitable." Purpose is needful in life. Not knowing the purpose of why something is made will lead to the improper use of that thing. Imagine a builder builds a house and hands over the keys to the person who is supposed to live in the house (purpose), instead of the person moving into the house, decides to stay outside so he won't dirty the place. In the same vein, a man spends his money to buy a brand new car but, seeing the beauty and sophistication of the vehicle, decides to keep the car at home while he uses a taxi or bike to move around. The reality here is that these people have actually abused the use of those products, i.e., the house and the car. House is meant for shelter and protection, while a vehicle is intended to ease your mobility. The need for purpose in any endeavour cannot be overemphasised.

Every good and successful life is hinged on a solid purpose. Show me a successful man in life and destiny, and I will show you a man with an unwavering purpose.

Purpose is a firm resolution of the outcome of a thing, translated into faith with which the world is built. You can't even please God without it. It is the fuel that energizes our actions. Heb 11:1 says faith is the substance (outcome) of the things hoped for (purpose). Purpose creates a strong faith. The joy of becoming a university graduate (purpose) will allow me to see the four, five, or six-year course with all its rigours as if it is nothing.

You can have a strong or a weak purpose. A strong purpose will produce strong, calculated, predictable, and desired outcomes, while a weak purpose will produce weak calculated outcomes and sometimes, no result. With a weak purpose, you may accomplish nothing at the end of the day.

> *"If any of you lack wisdom, let him ask of God, that giveth to all men liberally, and upbraideth not; and it shall be given to him, but let him ask in faith, nothing wavering. For he that wavereth is like a wave of the sea driven with the wind and tossed. For let not that man think that he shall receive anything of the Lord. A double-minded man is unstable in all his ways" (James 1:5-8, KJV).*

Purpose is essential for living. Great exploits both for God and in the natural have been done on the reality of solid purpose. The tower of Babel in Genesis chapter 11 couldn't have been built without a strong sense of purpose.

Life Without Purpose

When we imagine a life without purpose, then we imagine a man without a destination. He becomes aimless, a wanderer without a mission. Such life will never find fulfilment. Fulfilment is found in the purpose for which that thing exists.

Hosea 4:6 explains that people cast off restraints when there is no predefined purpose. We have all manners of abuse of creation today simply because of a lack of God-given purpose. The human innovations against the purpose of God who created man are examples to mention a few, such as in Rom 1:20.

> 'For the invisible things of him from the creation of the world are clearly seen, being understood by the things that are made, even his eternal power and Godhead; so that they are without excuse; because of that, when they knew God, they glorified him not as God, neither were thankful but became vain in their imaginations, and their foolish heart was darkened. Professing themselves to be wise, they became fools, and changed the glory of the incorruptible God into an image made like to corruptible man, and to birds, and four-footed beasts and creeping things, wherefore God also gave them up to uncleanness through the lusts of their own hearts, to dishonour their own bodies between themselves who changed the truth of God into a lie, worshipped and served the creature more than the creator who is blessed forever Amen. For this cause God gave them up to vile affections: for even their women did change the natural use into that which is against nature; And likewise also the men, leaving the natural use of women, burned into their lust one towards another, men with men working that which is unseemly, and receiving in themselves that recompense of their error which was meet" (KJV).

The reason for the illegalities, lawlessness and social vices today is the lack of universal purpose. One of the first chaos in the Bible was the building of the tower of Babel, which was a lack of God-given purpose.

The manufacturer of a product determines its purpose. That is why every new product comes with the manufacturer's manual to understand its purpose and operation. Life without purpose will lead to a careless, unrestrained, non-directional life, bringing us to a hasty doom.

The Impact Of Purpose On Earth

To God: When God created the world, He had a purpose in mind which He still longed to see. Let us see some scriptures that relate to an issue in the mind of God and how He intends to handle it.

> *"But as truly as I live, all the earth shall be filled with the glory of the Lord" (Num 14:21).*
>
> *"For the earth shall be filled with the knowledge of the glory of the Lord, as the waters cover the sea."Isa 11:9. "They shall not hurt nor destroyed in all my holy mountain: for the earth shall be full of the knowledge of the Lord as the waters cover the sea" (Hab 2:14).*
>
> *"And blessed be his glorious name forever: and let the whole earth be filled with his glory, Amen and Amen" (Ps 72:19).*
>
> *"And one cried unto another, and said, Holy, Holy, Holy is the Lord of hosts; the whole earth is full of his glory" (Isa 6:3).*

God's intention to fill the whole earth with His glory was differently mentioned five times in the above scriptures. This shows how absolute the word of God must be performed. Right from the beginning of time, the mind of God has been on the earth to produce His glory in the same dimension and frequency at which waters cover the sea. He has raised many people in different generations to accomplish this singular purpose. God is still waiting patiently to see His purpose fulfilled on earth.

To Humans: Great achievers of old had dreams which translated into purpose, that later became strong faith in them to achieve the things they did in their time. We must understand the essence of purpose and walk in its reality to take the baton to the next level or next generation. We had great men of unwavering purpose who fought for a course and achieved it because of resolute purpose in their hearts.

Thomas Edison had several setbacks from his family, including a few; he had a hearing impairment and academic disqualifications. But none of these could deter him from achieving greatness. Today, he is known as one of the foremost inventors and entrepreneurs that America has ever produced.

Nelson Mandela of South Africa had a strong desire to liberate his people from apartheid. He spent 27 years of his youthful life in jail for no wrong reason and was still ready for more until he saw his goal accomplished.

Dr. Martin Luther King (Jr.) of the USA fought for the emancipation of the black race even to the detriment of his life. The list goes on and on concerning people who had setbacks during their endeavours but refused to give up because of a strong purpose.

Effects Of A Strong Purpose

Here are some examples of some features that can result out of a strong purpose. ***Strong purpose produces patience to wait:*** Strong purpose in man's heart makes him wait for it no matter the time it takes. A journey of ten years in the life of a purposeful man is seen as a journey of few days. He is continuously longing for the result rather than the difficulties involved. Gen 29:20-29.

It Removes Doubt: Strong purpose clears every doubt in the heart of the man. A man of purpose does not see oppositions; instead, he sees opportunities. Joshua and Caleb eliminated the doubt of ever losing the battle of Jericho because the word of the Lord formed a strong purpose in their lives. They saw giants as bread for lunch.

It Gives Clarity And Focus: A man of strong purpose is a man of singularity with precision to his assignment. Apostle Paul said, ***'this one thing I do, forgetting those things behind me.'*** Phil 3:13. He is a man of single focus. He is so convinced about the matter that it forms an unwavering purpose in him.

It Strengthens Your Faith: Strong purpose in man stirs up the latent energy (faith) to achieve that purpose. This faith can be from God, the devil, or in man. This faith releases the last energy even when everyone has given up. It is faith that goes the extra mile.

It Creates An End In View: A well-analyzed and strong purpose sees the result even before the job is done. The Bible recorded that Jesus endured the pains, humiliation from people He created, and the disgrace of the death on the cross just because He saw the end in view, which is 'the joy that was set before Him to be made the Lord of all, both in heaven, on earth and beneath the earth. **Phil 2:5-11.**

It Enforces The Power Of Vision: A man of purpose is a man of vision. The purpose enables him to see beyond what others cannot see. He always looks for the next thing to accomplish and is never satisfied with the status quo. Curiosity always draws him to seek more information to achieve his purpose. Great scientists of renown have been people of a strong purpose. They had ideas to produce something, and amidst troubles and economic imbalance, they never stopped searching for ways to come up with solutions. His live is driven by that purpose.

It Makes You Obsessional: Strong purpose in man makes him uncomfortable anywhere he stays. Jesus repeatedly told His disciples that His meat is to do the works of Him who sent Him and finish it. He got to the temple of worship and saw people selling, He took a whip and drove away all of them, and it was recorded that the zeal of His Father's house has eaten him up. Purpose is all-consuming.

THE
PURPOSE
OF THE

CHURCH
ON EARTH

CHAPTER 2

DEFINING THE CHURCH

"......And to make all men see what is the fellowship of the mystery, which from the beginning of the ages has been hidden in God who created all things through Jesus Christ, to the intent that now the manifold wisdom of God might be made known by the Church to the principalities and powers in the heavenly places, according to the eternal purpose which He accomplished in Christ Jesus our Lord" (Eph 3:9–11).

The Church In The Mind Of God

The Church had existed in the mind of God long before He created the earth. The all-knowing God was aware that humanity would fall. So even before it happened, He made arrangements for redemption. This redemption is through a complete MAN—Jesus (the head) and the Church (the body). They are to restore humanity and the world's systems to God's original intent and plan even before the fall. Jesus and His Church have existed even before the foundation of the world to carry out this task. Through Genesis (the beginning), Jesus and His Church have existed and worked to fulfill that purpose.

In The Beginning

> *"And God said; 'Let us make man in our image, after our likeness: and let them have dominion over the fish of the sea and over the fowl of the air and over the cattle, and over all the earth, and over every creeping thing that creeps upon the earth'. So God created man in His own image, in the image of God created he him; male and female created he them. And God blessed them, and God said unto them, 'be fruitful, and multiply and replenish the earth, and subdue it: and have dominion over the fish of the sea, and over the fowl of the air, and over every living thing that moves upon the earth" (Gen 1: 26-28).*

God's idea from creation is to produce a people of His like that will govern all His works in its entirety. In the above scripture, God gave man responsibility and authority over all other creatures. God has always been interested in managing His vast estate called His kingdom through people by putting His Spirit and laws inside them to say and do what He would say and do if He is there. This set of people exerts His laws, philosophies, principles, characters in those areas He gives them to manage.

Right from Adam, the tiller of the ground (farmer), Enoch, Noah, Abraham, Joseph, Moses, Joshua, David, Daniel, and the rest, God has been on the journey to managing His creation through people. These people, at different capacities, carried a level of God's deposit depending on His attribute He wanted to manifest at that time.

The mandate God gave the man in the above scripture, which is to be fruitful, multiply, replenish, subdue, and dominate the creation, has been watered down to solely procreation which is one of the <u>least</u> of the purpose for the mandate. There is a greater purpose for the assignment, and even till now, God's heart is not yet at rest in finding a people that will fulfill that purpose.

The objective is that <u>God wants to put His seed inside a man</u> to <u>produce a people called the 'sons of God' that will subdue and dominate the earth</u>. If the purpose of that mandate is the normal procreation as often thought, then by now, the objective would have been achieved as we have over six billion people in the world today. Then the end would have ultimately come because every purpose has starting and ending date. But God not yet satisfied shows that there is more to it than procreation.

God has always wanted to incubate man to produce sons of God to fulfill the mandate written in Genesis 1:26-28. In a later chapter, we will discuss the quality of life and character this man and these sons will possess and how it will be produced.

The Ecclesia Of God (The Church)

I feel in my spirit somebody arguing that there is nothing called Church in the Old Testament. The first time Church was built was in Acts, in the New Testament, so why mention people like Abraham, Moses, David, and others as part of the Church. We have a wrong perception of what the Church means; that is why we think the Church started in the New Testament.

Can we read Acts 7:37-38 together?

> "This is that Moses, which said unto the children of Israel, A Prophet shall the Lord your God raise up unto you of your brethren, like unto me; him shall you hear. This is he, which was with the Church in the wilderness with the Angel (Jesus) which spoke to him in the Mount Sinai, and with our fathers."

If the scriptures call the bunch of Israelite sojourners the Church and Jesus the Angel that spoke with them on Mount Sinai, why can't we also say that Noah, Enoch, and the rest are part of the Church?

What Then Is The Church?

My friend and brother, Isaac Arikawe, dealt extensively with the meaning of the Church in his books called "The Dead Living Church" and "The True Church." Please find the book to read.

The word 'Church' came from the Greek Word Ekklesia,' which means **'the called out ones for a specific and unique goal by a herald.'** The Word came from two words: Ek, which means out of, and klesis, which means a calling (Kaleo, "to call). The Word Church has been in existence long before Jesus made the heroic statement which had become a significant statement in the Body of Christ today.

The statement is in Matt 16: 18, which says, "thou art Peter, upon this rock I will build my church; and the gates of hell shall not prevail against it." The underlined personal pronoun 'my' presupposes that the Church Jesus was building was a particular type amid many other types.

Before Jesus appeared on the scene, the Roman government had some people set aside to oversee the law and the people with their welfare. They sit as legal authorities in their jurisdiction to judge matters about their people. It was more like a political, social, and spiritual gathering. The people who belong to that caucus are often the well-respected and noble people in society, with proven integrity and accountability. They were most often chosen by the emperor, who is the highest person within the domain. Their duties were to judge matters concerning the law of the land in favour of the emperor who put them there (herald). They were policymakers, and their jurisdiction transcends all spheres of the life of the people.

In the classical days of Athens, the ecclesia was the convened assembly of people. It consisted of all the citizens who had not lost their civic rights. Apart from the fact that its decisions had to conform to the state's laws, its powers were unlimited in all intents and purposes. It has the following functions:

- To raise and allocate funds.

- To elect and dismiss magistrates.

- To direct the policy of the city or state.

- To declare war, make peace, contract treaties, and arrange allegiances.

- To elect generals and other military officers who ultimately were responsible for the conduct of military operations.

There are two great words of this circular ecclesia. They are **'equality and freedom.'** All had equal rights and duty to take part and consider matters of public interest.

When Jesus came into the scene, He needed to declare His ekklesia and show the difference between His and others, hence that heroic statement. Though the same in function but a change of allegiance.

From this understanding, the Church of Jesus was set up to look after the affairs of the people in accordance with the instruction of their Master- Jesus. With this, we know that we have missed the primary purpose in the mind of Jesus setting up the Church. Jesus intended to raise His Church above the commandments of men so that the gates of hell cannot overcome her. The Church that is supposed to be the highest decision-making body on earth, the only potentate and the seat of God's government, has now been reduced to a mere club and social gatherings where we display our wealth and oppress those who don't have.

The Church left God's original purpose for her and settled in mediocrity, competition, and unnecessary rivalries, which have degraded the Church's power. The Church that was supposed to be the pace-setter is now being led by the people she should be leading. No wonder the preacher was crying in **Eccl 10: 5-7** that there is evil in the land; servants (the people of the world) are riding on horses while princes (the Church) walk as servants upon the earth.

It is an abomination and evil for the life of the Church to go under while the world is floating above. God granted the Church the power of dominance and suppression at the beginning (Gen 1:28). Unfortunately, now we are being controlled by the traditions of men, influences of people, policies, and economic circumstances of the day. Oh! What a tragedy! In Isa 1:2-3, it was as if God was lamenting and calling the heavens and earth to bear witness of His people who has forgotten Him. It seemed that their Maker has an expectation of them which they never accomplished.

> *"Hear, O heavens, and give ear, O earth: for the Lord hath spoken, I have nourished and brought up children, and they have rebelled against me. The ox knows his owner, and the ass his master's crib but Israel does not know, my people does not consider" (KJV).*

God desires something from His Church, unfortunately, the Church doesn't seem to understand; instead, they sit down to play Church, organize clubs and welfare programs, leaving the heart of the Master-the Lord Jesus to bleed in pain. Hence, the ongoing search for those whose hearts will be knitted with His will to bring His needs to pass on earth.

> *"For the eyes of the Lord range throughout the earth to strengthen those whose hearts are fully committed to him. You have done a foolish thing, and from now on you will be at war" (2 Chron 16:9, NIV).*

The Dynamics Of The Church

Jesus saw how internally depraved was the Roman Empire. Regardless of their outward display of sophistication, they were deeply rooted in occultism, pretending to be saving people but indeed destroying the people created by God. Jesus then declared His Church with power on that platform but with a different spirit and absolute loyalty to the Father in heaven.

The Church of Jesus is supposed to confront and overcome the highest powers in the world then and now. It was in the surge of that conflict He established His Church. The first charge Jesus gave after declaring His Church was that the gates (imprint, influence, philosophies, etc.) of Hades and Hell (institutions of Babylon) should not prevail against her. With their powers, influence, and authority, the other classes of the Church will not overcome His Church.

The Church Jesus started is different from what we see and practice today in the world. The Church Jesus began was not a weekly religious gathering that meets every Sunday to clap hands, dance, and share testimonies of how we got our dream jobs, cars, buildings, miracles, the list continues. All these are desirable, but that is not the main essence of the Church. In the first place, who told you that you must meet every Sunday? The Bible only says we should not forsake the assembly of the brethren but must it be on Sundays? It can be any other day.

The Church of Jesus is a group of people called by God for a specific task to achieve loyalty to their herald Jesus and the benefit of humanity. It means that a group of engineers whose dedication and commitment is towards God with a specific task to benefit humankind is called Church. A group of medical professionals whose loyalty is unto God, deciding the spiritual and physical affairs of the people within their God-given jurisdiction for the betterment of the people is a Church. The Church could also be a group of market men and women, farmers or people with a common interest, gathering together in the name of Jesus and deciding the fate of the people and circumstances within their jurisdiction, working together for the common good. So it is in every field of human endeavour on earth.

Individuals within such groups do not need to look for another local assembly to belong. They don't need to work so hard trying to become a deacon or elder in a local congregation because they want to serve the Lord. You are serving the Lord with your allegiance towards God and benefit to humanity if only God has given you that profession in the first place.

Each spiritually unique, specific local assembly of the Church of Jesus Christ produces a flavour different from others, thereby eliminating competition and rivalries, knowing that each assembly grows to compliment the work of another assembly. This is the mind behind Eph

4:10-13, which talks about the Church attaining the 'unity of the faith, the knowledge of the Son of God and a perfect man on earth.

When we as the Body of Christ (the Church) create a new pathway in the spirit, bringing an alternative direction of how things are done in all the fields of human endeavour on earth, we can conveniently say we have completely fulfilled the above-quoted scripture. The Church cannot be naive to the world's systems and operations and claim that we are in charge.

The intent is for Jesus to be Lord in every sphere of life. The Church has to dazzle the principalities and powers in all fields with God's manifold (many-sided) wisdom. This will reduce to nothing the influence of the so-called 'pastors' and 'men of God' who gather crowds they don't have the spiritual capacity and mental insight to handle.

Every Church of Jesus is supposed to be a light to people in a specific direction. The aggregate of these sets of the Church will illuminate the world and dispel darkness. The Church cannot say we are in charge, or we have victory when occult men (warlords) have taken over our educational system, our legal, political, and civil services, to mention but a few.

Jesus noticed the power-play manifested in the world's system. He then declared that His Church would clean all those messes, overturn their wisdom, and raise a standard that will attract even the heavenly angels on the earth. Let us also remember that this earth is the Lord's, and His desire is to reclaim it from the prince of this world.

> " *The earth is the Lord's, and everything in it,the world, and all who live in it" (Ps 24:1, NIV).*

A businessperson who is a believer under the leadership of a pastor who knows nothing about his field of endeavour cannot help him in times of severe spiritual confrontation in his business. A scientist on the verge of technological innovation encounters a demonic interruption and then turns to his pastor, a novice and unlearned in the science of life and never knows the mystery (the battle between light and darkness) during innovation cannot help him. Even when God downloads the solution of the problem to the pastor as the head, he still would not understand. Instead, he will interpret it religiously to his benefit.

May I say this at this juncture that Jesus is not gathering the 'rejected' and 'no do wells' of this world as His leaders. He is not looking for flicky or unstable people who never amount to anything in life to become leaders of His people. You can come to God as nothing, empty, and rejected to be His children. However, before you qualify to be among His leaders, you must have grown into maturity manifesting the attributes of God. The leader must have developed skills and intelligence from the Lord. .

The Church of Jesus was birthed in the height of satanic assault through the institutions created by the powers in His days. It wasn't a weak or mediocre Church but a Church that could withstand any institution that opposes her. The Church of Jesus was brought forth to take over and not sit around dialogging with people who oppose her. Jesus made an unequivocal statement at the declaration of His Church that the gates of hell shall not prevail (overpower, overcome, over-ride, or stop) His Church. This automatically means there will be confrontation, provocation, opposition, and rebellion against the Church. The Church is light in the midst of darkness. There is a constant attempt of the world system to distort, twist, and ultimately quench this light so that people won't understand its essence.

We have serious problems when our pastors and men of God are novices to the spiritual, mental, and emotional issues they grapple with.

> *"Woe (cursed, disgraced) to thee, O land (the Church), when thy king (pastor and leader) is a child (novice), and thy princes (ministers) eat in the morning (no spiritual or mental direction)! But blessed art thou, O land when your king is a son of nobles (of an excellent character), and thy princes eat in due season (accuracy, elevated sight), for strength and not for drunkenness!"(Eccl 10:16-17).*

The Church is supposed to be a solution provider to people's problems and not confuse them with that religious form of solution like a hungry man meeting a 'man of God' who then prayed for him to be filled in Jesus' name. After that, he asks the man to sow a 'seed faith' from the little he has, that God will multiply it. The so-called 'man of God' does not have any clue about the man's problem. The 'man of God' is an opportunist seeking to solve his poverty problem, taking undue advantage of the one who has come for help. This is why we see the multiplication of Churches everywhere without a recognized and ethical leadership from God. Some might say,' but Elijah requested for the last meal of the widow of Zarephath'; yes, its true. It only happened once as God wanted to interrupt the normal proceedings just to teach us His supernatural provision. Such doesn't happen all the time and so can't be a tradition or a doctrine as many do today.

The Lord Jesus Christ engaged a crowd of about 5000 men, excluding women and children who were hungry. He knew their spiritual, mental, psychological and physical needs, and He took care of them.

The Church Through Transition

Right from the beginning, God has desired to see His will and intentions accomplished on earth. He always declares His intention through the Prophetic instrument of His Church, which is the extension of His Kingdom on earth.

Amos 3:7 says, *"Surely the Lord God does nothing unless He first reveals His mind to His servants the prophet."*

God reveals His will per time as He deems fit, and not all at once so that man can fully comprehend and ultimately appropriate His purposes. The plans and purposes of God are in stages or what we call dispensations, and each can be called a season of refreshing from the Lord.

> *"Repent therefore and be converted, that your sins may be blotted out, so that times of refreshing may come from the presence of the Lord; and that He may send Jesus Christ, who was preached to you before, whom heaven must receive until the times of restoration of all things which God has spoken by the mouth of all His holy prophets since the world began" (Acts 3:19-21, NKV).*

> *"Now change your mind and attitude to God and turn to him so he can cleanse away your sins and send you wonderful times of refreshment from the presence of the Lord and send Jesus your Messiah back to you again. For he must remain in heaven until the final recovery of all things from sin, as prophesied from ancient times." (Act 3:19-21, TLB).*

> *"Repent ye therefore, and turn again, that your sins may be blotted out, that so there may come seasons of refreshing from the presence of the Lord; and that he may send the Christ who hath been appointed for you, (even) Jesus: whom the heaven must receive until the times of restoration of all things, whereof God spoke by the mouth of His holy prophets that have been from of old" (Act 3:19-21, ASV).*

The first thing to note in this scripture is that there are times of refreshing. The refreshing comes not at once but in phases. Refreshing is the dew from heaven (the manner from above) representing His resources, His gifts, His principles, philosophies, characters, and all that He represents at that moment in time. This refreshing dew has been coming from God's presence right from the beginning to this present time and will continue until the Church becomes fully matured to represent God fully on earth.

From the above scripture, Jesus will not come until the complete restoration of God's resources to transform us like Him ultimately. God's intention is clear. He wants the whole earth immersed by His principles, and the agent through which He will carry out this work is His Church. This restoration can be called the dispensations of God, the move of God, reformation, the list continues.

If there is a disorder from the original form, restoration or reformation is inevitable. The word 'reformation' (Greek: diorthosis) means to make a structural adjustment, straighten that which is broken, misshapen, protrude, or has become misaligned. It is to put back in the correct order or form. From the beginning of creation, the reformation process has been going on and will continue until all the words of the Lord are fulfilled, then Jesus will return. The most interesting thing here is that the Church is in the epicenter of this transitional move of God called reformation or restoration.

There are different phases of reformation. Each phase emphasizes a particular truth God was restoring which is a buildup of that already restored. Through this, the

Body of Christ grows until the fullness of God is attained. Let's identify a few of the many phases of reformation or restoration God has accomplished over time to fulfill His purpose on earth.

PHASE ONE- Reformation In Creation

"In the beginning, God created the heavens and the earth. The earth was without form, and void; and darkness was on the face of the deep. And the spirit of God was hovering over the face of the waters. Then God said, "Let there be Light, and there was Light" (Genesis 1:1-2).

There is a big gap between verses one and two of the above scripture. In verse one, God created the heavens and the earth in a perfect state. Everything was good until Lucifer, the Arc angel of God, disobeyed by desiring the throne of God. (Isa 14:12-20; Ezek 28:1-19). He (Lucifer) was then thrown down to the earth, which caused the disorder in verse two of the scripture. From then, Lucifer, who later turns to become the devil and Satan, started distorting the plans of God.

This incident necessitated the first restoration, a series of activities initiated by heaven to bring things back to the original design. There was the restoration of the earth with order, governance, structure, and hierarchy. There was the restoration of the dignity of man: his spiritual powers, intelligence, mental capabilities, emotional and psychological influence on earth.

PHASE TWO – Reformation In The Shift From The Old Covenant To The New Covenant

"The Holy Spirit indicating this, that the way into the Holiest of All was not yet made manifest while the first tabernacle was still standing. It was symbolic for the present time in which both gifts and sacrifices are offered, which cannot make him who performed the service perfect in regard to the conscience – concerned only with foods and drinks, various washing and fleshly imposed until the time of reformation" (Heb 9:8-10).

There is another massive movement in the Church from the way we worship in terms of sacrifices. The priests wearing their priestly robes for sacrifice was no longer necessary as those things are now pointing to the personality of our Lord Jesus, who now lives inside of us.

Jesus has now become the ultimate sacrificial lamb. Therefore, the ceremonial washings, killing of goats, and the high priest going into the Holiest of all once a year are now abolished and made obsolete. All those requirements have been fulfilled in Christ. The laws of God are now written in our hearts, no more in tables of stone. The concern now becomes the essence of those sacrifices and the priestly robes incarnated in us to become values we uphold. The death and resurrection of our Lord Jesus Christ have now made a new way. The curtain demarcating the entrance to the Holy of Holies is now torn apart, giving us free access into the very presence of God. We no longer need a human priest to mediate between God and us. We can approach and interact with God directly on a one-on-one basis. Giving our lives to Christ now elevates us into the priesthood status, thereby giving us access to the holiest place. What an opportunity!

PHASE THREE - Restoration Of The Body Ministry (5 – Fold Ministry)

When God declared the restoration of all things through the mouth of Apostle Peter in Acts 3:19, He meant it in its entire ramification. He was declaring that the Church will have a set of leaders and functioning spirits that will govern the Church until she gets to her full maturity as it is said in Ephesians 4:7-13,

> *"But unto every one of us is given grace according to the measure of the gift of Christ. Wherefore he said, when he ascended up on high, he led captivity captive, and gave gifts unto men. Now that He ascended, what is it but that he also descended first into the lower parts of the earth. He that descended is the same also that ascended up far above the heavens, that he might fill all things. And he gave some apostles; and some prophets and some evangelists and some pastors and teachers; for the perfecting of the saints, for the work of the ministry, for the edifying of the body of Christ; till we all come in the unity of the faith, and of the knowledge of the son of God, unto a perfect man, unto the measure of the stature of the fullness of Christ."*

We have the five-fold ministry functions of the Holy Spirit released on the Church at different times to nurture the Church to grow and mature into sonship, to execute God's purposes on earth. They are the evangelists, the teachers, the pastors, the prophets, and the apostles. Each of these functions is a grace released to build the Church. The purpose is not about the person endowed with the gift but the entire Church which God has in mind to establish. The Church is to receive the resources which that grace represents.

The first restoration after the era of the acts of the Apostles was the reformation led by Martin Luther. This led to the Protestant Reformation, which ushered in an evangelistic spirit to the Body of Christ and drew a massive number of people into the Church. This was after the apostate Roman Catholic Church drifted away from the gospel's truth in the 14th century.

When this grace is released, God intended the whole Church to key into it by becoming evangelistic in all her approach to things about the kingdom. This grace witnessed Martin Luther, the Wesley brothers, William Tyndale, Billy Graham, and a lot more. When a new grace is released, it comes with its new operations, new lifestyle, new songs, etc., unique to that grace.

In response to the declaration of Peter, God released another grace, the pastoral spirit. This stirred up compassion and love towards one another, in and beyond the Church. The care of the Body of Christ became prevalent. Assemblies were bearing names as 'Christ Family Church,' Love World,' to mention a few. This outpouring of the pastoral grace started shaping the love of God among brethren and ultimately bringing God's kind of love to the dying world.

After that, God restored the teaching grace during Kenneth Hagin (Sr.) of blessed memory, James Gordon Lindsay of Christ, for the Nations Institute and their likes. God used them in restoring His truth to the Body of Christ- the exegesis of His Word, explaining the scripture systematically and with much profundity and clarity. This was the season of the 'Faith Movement.' This grace guided the Church to the revelation knowledge of God's promises in the Bible. During this dispensation, the Church became more conscious of the unseen promises of God in the Bible.

The next after the teaching is the Prophetic Grace that brought direction to the Church, making her come alive with the Living Word of the Lord. The teaching grace concentrates on God's written (logos) Word, but the Prophetic focuses on God's spoken (Rhema) Word. Both are very important to the existence of the Church. God used the Prophetic to point the Church to Himself and not to prosperity, miracles, and other things that people seek. This grace is designed to make the Church Prophetic, hearing from God and responding to His instructions. It points the Church to the next agenda of God on earth. This agenda is in all fields of human endeavors.

At present, God is releasing the Apostolic Grace to the Church for strength, direction, and breakthrough. This is a breakthrough and pioneering anointing. It is a finishing anointing. Please permit me to dwell on this a little bit. Like I said before, the release is not about the person functioning in the office of an Apostle but the grace of apostleship released to the Body of Christ so we can grow to perfection.

The Apostle is essential in the release, but the emphasis is the people – the Body of Christ that becomes Apostolic in nature, lifestyle, operations, and structure. Right from the reformation that started with Martin Luther in the 1500s, God has been adding layers of ingredients necessary for the Church to be perfect and come to manifest the word of Eph 4:12- 13. Apostleship talks about the foundation and pillar of the Church. Eph 2:20 'And are built upon the foundation of the apostle & prophets, Jesus Christ himself being the chief cornerstone.'

It has to do with structure, the framework of the body. The Apostolic grace deals with our character, inner lifestyle, and also the dominion of God.

All these seasons are not without challenges, counterfeits, and attacks from the older moves. Check out our book on 'The Five-fold Ministry' for more details.

It is said about the five-fold ministry that the feet represent the Evangelistic, the heart represents the Pastoral, the tongue represents the teaching, the voice (mouth) represents the Prophetic, while the hand represents the Apostolic.

Isa 9:6 says the government of God will rest upon his shoulder (part of the hand), which signifies responsibility for the Apostolic Church.

In these last days, the Prophetic and the Apostolic grace will become prevalent in the Church to rebuild the new heaven and new earth and enforce the reign and dominion of God on earth.

In the same way, when the cloud moved in the wilderness, everybody moved in the direction of the cloud. Now, when the Spirit of the Lord moves, the whole Church is expected to move towards His direction. Consequently, anyone who refused to move in the wilderness was either killed by the enemies, eaten by wild animals, or starved to death, so it is also in our days. Ministries and individuals die and go into extinction when they refuse to move to the next level with God when He moves.

Please note that any new move God brings on earth is an addition to what He has already brought previously. It does not mean the abandonment of the old but addition and a switch in direction and emphasis.

Each season produces a whole new lifestyle, structures, and operations, with new ministries and accompanying grace. The detail is outside the scope of this book.

The Role Of The Apostolic Church In Building The New Earth As Prophesied

"And I have put my words in thy mouth (Prophetic), and I have covered in the shadows of mine hand (Apostolic), that I may plant the heavens, and lay the foundations of the earth, and say unto Zion, thou art my people" (Isa 51:16).

The Lord is laying the foundation of the new earth and planting the new heaven using the Apostolic and Prophetic ministry. The Lord is changing the order of worship, the Levitical priesthood, the kingly activities through the Apostolic and Prophetic grace. It's a whole structural overhaul.

The extremisms of the older moves of God derailed the Church from her original purpose on earth, which is why God is bringing a total structural change. We must embrace the change for us to align with the speaking of God for now. When God declares the new, He makes the old obsolete. When God finishes His restructuring work in the Church, He will use the Apostolic Church to enforce His will on earth. It's an awesome move. Please see our book to understand its impact on the Church and the world.

The Saint Movement

There is another move that will come after the Apostolic move, which is called the Saint Movement. This is when the Church must have gotten to the status of Ephesians 4:13. God needed a few remnants of believers to get to this status to kick start this move. These remnants will be the ones that will bring millions into the kingdom of God. At that time, the five-fold ministry will leave the center stage for these matured saints who will do exploits for God's kingdom. This move will herald the coming of the Lord Jesus. It's a highly provocative move to the kingdom of darkness. These saints will preach the so-called 'everlasting gospel,' that will sweep multitudes from across the globe into the kingdom of God. Their principal duty is to unseat Satan and his cohorts in all ramifications and fields of human endeavour, where they are illegally occupying. These matured saints must undergo all the disciplines of God and know what He wants in every circumstance. They will be spread across every field of human endeavor. The motive is to please their Master Jesus even when harmful to their own lives, not even talk about their loved ones. Their activities will be very swift and short, bringing blessings and judgments to nations. Their judgment will be almost as accurate as God's.

The Final Phase of Reformation

The final phase will be the renovation of heaven and earth- all things made new.

'Now I saw a new heaven and a new earth, for the first heaven and the first earth had passed away. Also there was no more sea. Then I, John, saw the holy city, New Jerusalem, coming down out of heaven from God, prepared as a bride adorned for her husband. And I heard a loud voice from heaven saying, "Behold, the tabernacle of God is with men, and He will dwell with them, and they shall be His people. God Himself will be with them and be their God. And God will wipe away every tear from their eyes; there shall be no more death, nor sorrow, nor crying. There shall be no more pain, for the former things have passed away. Then He who sat on the throne said, "Behold, I make all things new." And He said to me, "Write, for these words are true and faithful." And He said to me, "It is done! I am the Alpha and the Omega, the Beginning, and the End. I will give of the fountain of the water of life freely to him who thirsts. He who overcomes shall inherit all things, and I will be his God, and he shall be My son. But the cowardly, unbelieving, abominable, murderers, sexually immoral, sorcerers, idolaters, and all liars shall have their part in the lake which burns with fire and brimstone, which is the second death" (Rev 21:1-7, NKJV).

This new heaven and earth will now become the abode of God Himself. There will be no gap between heaven and earth as the activities within them will be seamless. It will be like it was in the Garden of Eden before Adam sinned. It is a life where there will be no sun, moon, day, or night anymore, but the glory and light coming from the presence of God will be the light forever.

THE PURPOSE OF THE CHURCH ON EARTH

CHAPTER 3

WHAT THE CHURCH IS NOT

We understood in the previous chapter that God established the Church for a unique purpose. The Church does not exist for herself but for the pleasure of He who established her. The Church that Jesus Christ is the head of has some attributes that differentiate her from the synagogue of Satan.

Some Attributes Cannot Be Seen In The Church Of Jesus

Any church whose **ideologies and the main emphasis** are based on the following points we will discuss in the succeeding paragraphs is not the Church of Jesus. Instead, a social club or gathering or that of the Anti-Christ.

The Church Is Not A Physical Structure

From what we have seen in our previous chapters, the Church is a body of believers of Jesus Christ whose lifestyle is represented by their herald-the Lord Jesus. This means that the components of the Church had to do with the values in the life of Jesus. Building a physical structure or a cathedral is not wrong if the purpose is to accommodate believers so that the purpose of God will be achieved.

But if the attention and glory are ascribed to the building, it's no longer God. The building is nothing without the people who made up the Church. The size and the artistic designs of the building do not measure the spiritual condition of the Church. However, the impact the people make within the society concerning the God-given purpose for them within the global purpose of God for the entire Church should be the yardstick to measure the Church's growth.

Some people measure the spiritual growth of a church based on how the church's building is rated, the brand of cars parked at the church's parking garage, the brand and quality of suits the ministers wear, how the church services are structured, and the sophistication of the environment, etc., without taking into account the spiritual impact the church makes in her community. Unfortunately, these are not God's metrics to measure spiritual growth.

Every local assembly is unique in its purpose and operation, depending on the ability God gives them. So the yardstick to measure should be based on their response to God's vision and mandate to that local assembly and not these transitory and mundane things.

Again, no part of the church building is holier than the other. What makes it holy or sacred is that the people of God are there. You become righteous once you accept Jesus into your life because the holy God now lives in you. God no longer dwells in the building made with human hands. He resides in our hearts as believers. On no ground should we adore the building more than the people living in it. That was the Old Testament order when the glory of God would descend upon the tent (house) where the people assembled. At such moments, whatever is unclean that touches the temple is killed.

The temple (worship place) was always a sacred place. When people come to worship, they purify themselves to meet with God. They had to behave piously to avoid the wrought of God. The scripture below is a description of the scenario in the Old Testament:

> *"And the Lord said to Moses, Go into the people, and sanctify them today and tomorrow, and let them wash their clothes, and be ready against the third day: for the third day the Lord will come down in the sight of all the people upon Mount Sinai. And thou shall set bounds unto the people round about, saying, Take heed to yourselves, that ye go not up into the mount, or touch the border of it: whoever toucheth the mount shall be surely put to death"* (Exo 19:10-12).

In the New Testament order, after Jesus died and was resurrected, He changed the law from the table of stones to the hearts of men. He then declared that the believers are now His temple.

> *"Not according to the covenant that I made with their fathers in the day when I took them by the hand to lead them out of the land of Egypt; because they continued not in my covenant, and I regarded them not, says the Lord. For this is the covenant that I will make with the house of Israel after those days, says the Lord: I will put my laws into their mind, and write them in their hearts: and I will be to them a God, and they shall be to me a people"* (Heb 8:9-10).

Again, I Cor 3:16 says;

> *"Know ye not that ye are the temple of God, and that the spirit of God dwells in you?"*

Again, comparing a believer with an unbeliever by calling us the temple of God He said in II Cor 6:16,

> *"And what agreement has the temple of God with idols? For you are the temple of the living God; as God has said, I will dwell in them, and walk in them: I will be their God, and they shall be my people.*

God has now shifted His emphasis from that physical temple to the spiritual temple that is now our hearts where God dwells. God wants it to be holy and sacred the same way He intended the physical temple to be holy back then in the wilderness. The physical temple becomes a shadow of reality, which is the heart of believers.

Finally, on this issue, a scripture says, we know no man after the flesh anymore. What counts for any local assembly is your impact in the spirit, your worth in the things God has assigned you to do. We need to be divine in our operations.

The Church Is Not For Displaying Wealth, Power, Gifts, Talents, And Knowledge

Rom 14:17 says,

> *"The kingdom of God is not meat and drink; righteousness, peace, and joy in the Holy Ghost."*

The Church of Jesus Christ should not be displaying material wealth like cars, houses, and social status as proof of God's validation. It is not a place to show off power, those who have more anointing or influence in society. Neither is it a place to flaunt your gifts, comparing who has more spiritual gifts than the others. We don't come to church to know who is more talented, knowledgeable, intelligent, materially wealthier, and wiser to attract the crowd. As much as these things mentioned above might be needed to advance the kingdom, one principal fact is that the Holy Spirit must lead the Church, not any of those things or our intuition.

The Lord can either decide to use or not use any of these things to advance His purpose. The Bible recorded that all we do in the kingdom is considered a seed we plant, but God gives the seed a body according to how IT PLEASES HIM. He chooses which is necessary and which is not. We are mere tools in His hands, so there is nothing to glory about.

The main reason most people in Church come to God is for Him to prosper them. So about 90% of their prayers and activities to God are geared toward receiving material blessings from Him. They insist that He must bless them materially. When they are blessed with financial and other material resources, they wear them as a badge to prove that God is with them. They go around bragging with some cliche like 'my God is not a poor God,' 'God desires that you should prosper and be in health even as your soul prospers,' 'God has given us the riches of the gentiles,' 'through prosperity, the gospel will be preached,' etc.

I don't have problems with these quotes, and also, I am not a preacher of poverty either. Poverty is not in me. But we must understand the context of the scriptures we quote, and not contradict them with some other scriptures. When we take a scripture out of context, we miss the essence and later realize that other places in the scriptures contradict what we say or preach.

God is interested in the prosperity of His people but for a purpose. The world has not yet known the true riches which is coming to believers for kingdom advancement. The world will be amazed at the magnitude and dimension of God's recourses that will come to the remnant Church in this end time. Authentic and enduring wealth is coming that will terrify the world.

But let's analyze some things here. Do we need God to be rich in this world? Is that the purpose of sending His Son to die? If it's true, why do unbelievers become wealthy? Why is it that some occultic and evil people in this world are wealthy while most believers are not? The wealthiest people in the world today are not people who know God.

The fact is that riches are governed by the natural laws or principles of 'seedtime and harvesttime.' If you obey the laws and principles governing success and prosperity, you become wealthy irrespective of knowing God or not. Someone who has an MBA with solid knowledge of financial management and a desire to succeed will thrive in business regardless of who the person is.

If this is the case, the question is, 'where is the place of God in the life of a believer concerning prosperity and success?

Jesus came that He might destroy the power of servitude, which Babylon and darkness have lorded over humanity. Therefore, Jesus can give us the power (wisdom & creative instinct) to produce things on earth in His ways.

The gripe of Babylon on humanity has turned our eyes away from seeing riches in God's perspectives. We need fervent prayers, teaching, and a mental shift to get us out of the hold that darkness has over the people of God, so we can think and act the way God thinks and acts. Without this power of God, we can make money but will not be different from Babylon in terms of how we pursue riches and success.

We will always see riches, wealth as something to chase after and accumulate, something that owns us, something that we cannot do without, and something that we must get.

No wonder it reflects in the way we go about it and display it whenever we get it.

A local assembly will spend valuable time teaching people how to be rich instead of teaching them how to exercise power inherent in them from God to overcome the grip of Babylon. When we learn the principle of success, we can apply it in God's ways to create wealth. We should teach people the morals and values of the kingdom. Our business schools do even more than that. We eventually end up doing it in Babylon's way. Babylon thrives on competition, survival of the fittest, rivalry, and the divide and rule game. Babylon will always want to show off (display) whatever she has. She is always the people's choice but not God's choice.

These scriptures below well explain this point:

> *"Ye adulterers and adulteresses, know ye not that the friendship of this world is enmity with God? Whosoever, therefore, will be a friend of the world is an enemy of God. Do you think the scripture saith in vain, the Spirit that dwells in us lusteth to envy?" (James 4:4-5).*

> *"Love not the world neither the things that are in the world. If any man loves the world, the love of the Father is not in him. For all that is in the world, the lust of the flesh, the lust of the eyes, and the pride of life is not of the Father but of the world. The world passeth away, and the lust thereof: but he that does the will of God abides forever" (1John 2:15-17).*

The world in these scriptures talks about the system of operation and principles that govern how society. Two people can carry out the same task, get the same result but with different processes. However, we are in the world, but we are not of the world. We might get the same result in the world in terms of accomplishments, but our processes and sources must differ. In the schemes of God, the result is not always what matters. What counts is the process and the source.

The spirit and principles of Babylon have been enshrined in the Church today. There is too much display of our wealth, power, gift, and knowledge in the Church. It has almost become like a marketplace where everybody seeks recognition and popularity. Would you please read what the Lord Jesus admonished concerning these things in Matt 6:1-6?

> *"Be especially careful when you are trying to be good so that you don't make a performance out of it. It might be good theatre, but the God who made you won't be applauding. When you do something for someone else, don't call attention to yourself. You have seen them in action, I'm am sure- 'play actors' I call them – treating prayer meeting and street corner alike as a stage, acting compassionate as long as someone is watching, playing to the crowds. They get applause, true, but that's all they get. When you help someone out, don't think about how it looks. Just do it- quietly and unobtrusively. That is the way your God, who*

conceived you in love, working behind the scenes, helps you out. And when you come before God, don't turn that into a theatrical production either. All these people making a regular show out of their prayers, hoping for stardom! Do you think God sits in a box seat? Here's what I want you to do: find a quiet, secluded place so you won't be tempted to role-play before God. Just be there as simply and honestly as you can manage. The focus will shift from you to God, and you will begin to sense his grace" (THE MSG).

Understand me to say that God is interested in the riches of His people. He is highly interested even more than we are but with the right motive and without the hold of Babylon and darkness attached.

God will be releasing in this end-time hidden riches that the world has not tapped into yet. He will be unleashing His power, gifts, divine knowledge that surpasses human intelligence that will startle the nations of the earth. However, this is exclusively reserved for His kingdom saints who would use these resources to advance the kingdom of God and nothing more.

God would have chastised them so much in the school of the Holy Ghost that the glory and the glamour of Babylon could not grip them. You can only hear such words as these from them. Give me the whole world; it will not shift my gaze upon God,' 'put the nations under my command, it will not change my pursuit,' I am a conduit pipe through which the blessings of God flow.' And after I have done the will of Master, I will say, I am an unprofitable servant.' (Please read Deut. 8:18; Isa 45:1-3).

But wait a minute, are we just hearing this now, or has it been said before? Is our riches meant for other people or us? Is it meant for display? What can we speak of the biblical heroes of the faith (champions of God) in Heb 11? some of whom the Bible recorded that they wondered in goat skins meanwhile they were too good for the earth; what can we say of our Lord Jesus Himself who was very rich yet was seen as very poor for the sake of the gospel; what about Apostle Paul who was seen as poor yet making many rich.

From where did we fall into this deadly deception of accessing people based on their natural disposition and not from God's point of view? All these are results of what our hearts are longing for. We are so obsessed with acquiring riches, spiritual power, and gifts, leaving the Giver because of the sinful nature of our hearts. The Bible says, "…he that maketh haste to be rich shall not be innocent" Prov 28:20. We are so interested in heaven without knowing the owner of the heaven we clamour for. This is Babylon, my dear friend; no matter the result, we get out of it.

The Church Is Not A Business Venture

"The Passover of the Jews was near, and Jesus went up to Jerusalem. And He found in the temple those who were selling oxen and sheep and doves, and the money-changers seated at their tables. And He made a scourge of cords, and

drove them all out of the temple, with the sheep and the oxen; and He poured out the coins of the money-changers and overturned their tables; and to those who were selling the doves He said, "Take these things away; stop making My Father's house a place of business." His disciples remembered that it was written, "ZEAL FOR YOUR HOUSE WILL CONSUME ME" (John 2:13-17, NASU).

"So they came to Jerusalem. Then Jesus went into the temple and began to drive out those who bought and sold in the temple and overturned the tables of the money-changers and the seats of those who sold doves. And He would not allow anyone to carry wares through the temple. Then He taught, saying to them, "Is it not written, 'My house shall be called a house of prayer for all nations. But you have made it a den of thieves" (Mark 11:15-17, NKJV).

"Also the sons of the foreigner who join themselves to the Lord, to serve Him, and to love the name of the Lord, to be His servants. Everyone who keeps from defiling the Sabbath and holds fast My covenant, even them I will bring to My holy mountain, and make them joyful in My house of prayer. Their burnt offerings and their sacrifices will be accepted on My altar; For My house shall be called a house of prayer for all nations" (Isaiah 56:6-7, NKJV).

The scriptures above are the accounts of the same event recorded by two different people. The most exciting part was what the Lord Jesus did when He arrived at the temple. Some people still mistake this to mean not to change money for offering in the Church. What Jesus demonstrated is far more than the issue of offering. He came and changed the old religious order and structure that was in operation before His arrival.

At that time, worshippers in the temple in Israel were required to buy cattle, sheep, doves, pigeons for sacrifices. These people come from far to worship or for atonement, so the priests request that they use the blood of a goat, sheep, or any other for sacrifice. They have to buy the things for the sacrifice at the temple. They also have people who exchange money from one currency to another for worshippers in the temple. All these were legitimate practices right from the time of Moses, and it's been going on long before Jesus came.

People come from all over the world to offer sacrifices in the temple at Jerusalem, so the priests saw it as a business opportunity to start an Animal Husbandry and Currency Exchange Business. It became a lucrative venture that the higher your pay, the higher your sacrifice, and consequently, the more prayers you will receive from the priests. As the event continued, they no longer accepted any sacrificial animals not bought from them in the temple. They organised themselves as a union to advance their merchandising.

Amid that commercial activities, Jesus walked into the temple during the Passover to pray. When He saw those events going on, He became outraged, went aside, got a strong cord, made a whip out of it, then went after those sellers and buyers. He fought them single-handedly until He drove all of them out of the temple.

Let me ask a question, 'do you think that immediately Jesus brought out the whip, all the sellers and buyers quickly ran away without any form of resistance? Remember that this has become their means of livelihood to support their families and loved ones. Jesus was just an ordinary man like them, as a son of Mary. I am sure they would have resisted Him, but Jesus overpowered them. No wonder the disciples who were with Him then remembered a scripture written about Him which says, *'The zeal of His Father's house has consumed Him.'* What they were doing in the temple was permissible in the days of Moses, but in the time of Jesus, it is no longer accepted. The order has changed.

Most times, we, as kingdom believers, cannot stand against a truth that has become obsolete just because it is acceptable to the crowd or what we will lose when it is gone. Would you please let that same scripture that the disciple saw about Jesus be manifested in your life? Amen.

Having driven the sellers away in the temple, Jesus made a compelling statement which is the main subject of this sub-topic. He told them that it was already written in their books that *'My house shall be called a house of prayers for all nations',* but they have turned it to be a den of robbers.

From that statement again, the Church made some

mistakes by organizing prayer meetings, thinking that the prayers were not enough and God wanted the Church to focus more on prayers. Prayer is good, and its efficacy cannot be over-emphasized. But Jesus was more mindful of a higher essence than prayer. He was introducing a new order as initiated by the Father in Isaiah 56.

God intended that His house be called a house of prayers for all nations and not a den of robbers. But the people turned His house into a den of robbers. This is a very significant component of the Kingdom of God. It explains why for the first time, Jesus took a whip against them. If it provoked Jesus to the point of organizing a whip against a crowd, it should also concern us if we are indeed from Him.

We need to critically look into what becoming a 'den of robbers' means and what it means to be a 'house of prayers for all nations.' Who was Jesus referring to as the 'den of robbers? They were the sellers and buyers in the temple. But let us analyze this critically. Were they stealing to the extent that Jesus referred to them as the den of robbers? They were helping to make sacrifices and worship easier for visitors coming from different parts of the world. That is true, but Jesus was pointing at something more than that.

Jesus referred to some people as the den of robbers, and some others as the house of prayers for the nations. These two sets of people are in our churches today. Their titles or their gifts do not identify them, but their lifestyles do. We intend to compare both to reveal these two sets and trust the Holy Spirit of God to lead His Church to become a house of prayer for the nations of the earth as intended.

Church of House of Prayers	Church of Den of Robbers
The word 'prayer' denotes giving out something. A people that gives.	The word 'robber' denotes one who collects but never gives out. A people that always ask.
It is a prayer for the development of all nations (people groups), not just for self. It is a selfless people.	It is a prayer meanly for himself, his business, job, and his church. Just self. A selfish and self-centered people.
Their activities are without a price (Jesus has paid the price). A God-seeking people. Here, people give willingly without being cajoled.	Their activities towards the people are always with a price, a seed, and a compulsory offering.
Here, anointing is according to the leading of the Holy Ghost.	The higher your pay (seed offering, gifts) to the 'man of God,' the higher the anointing that flows to you.
It is a service to God for humanity and not vice versa. They seek their reward from God and not from the person that has benefited from the service. God blesses with whomsoever, and however, He wishes.	It is purely a service to man using God's resources, so man must pay at his expense using any means defined by the giver.
Sincerely, their activities are always God's conscious, asking what does God say about the matter?	Their activities are always people/self-conscious, asking what happens to my ministry, church, reputation, etc. It is all about self.

What Jesus did in the temple at Jerusalem was to establish the Church as the house of prayer where nations of the earth would come for safety and security and not be defrauded by false miracles, signs, and wonders designed to reap them of their resources. This Church is emerging, and she is already here in Jesus' name. Amen.

THE
PURPOSE
OF THE

CHURCH
ON EARTH

CHAPTER 4

COMPONENTS OF THE CHURCH

The Church that the Lord Jesus built has several components. Each of these components must be noticed in every kingdom believer's life and our local assemblies in general. Though you may not be fully established in all of them, you should have traces of these elements in your life because they are the intrinsic attributes of our God.

Let us examine some of the attributes.

The Church As The Body Of Christ

I want to start by saying it is not our body or the body of the head pastor or general overseer. It is the Body of Christ our Lord. Most times, we forget to understand that Jesus is the Head of the Church. We may know it in our head without a corresponding action in our day-to-day life. If we do, the majority of the perversion prevalent today will not have been.

The meaning of the headship in the Church is that Jesus is in charge of the body's activities, which is the Church, and He should give direction on how we conduct activities. Notice what the scriptures say about someone under the leadership and authority of another person. The Church should follow this same principle.

> "I tell you the truth; the Son can do nothing by himself; he can only do what he sees his Father doing because whatever the Father does, the Son also does. For the Father loves the Son and the shows him all he all he does. Yes, to your amazement, he will show him even greater things than these....By myself, I can do nothing; I judge only as I hear, and my judgement is just for I seek not to please myself but him who sent me" (John 5:19-30).

In the scripture above, Jesus explained the practical reality of what headship and sonship are all about. Jesus is the head, while the Church as His body is required to follow His will. The Church is meant to do nothing of herself but instead listens and obeys her master Jesus's will from this scripture. As humans, we are often prone to activities. This is also one of the things Babylon thrives on. She places preference on continual activity. Babylon lures humanity to depend on self rather than on God, his maker.

From the beginning of creation until now, God never intended to do anything except what He shows us. The head contains the brain, where all responses come from. The brain controls all the activities within the body, so also is the Church (body) to Jesus that functions as the brain. The Church is supposed to be like the waiter in the restaurant waiting for orders. He does nothing of his own will except by instruction.

Again, the Church must have enough insight to see what Jesus is showing her at each time so she can implement it on earth to advance the Kingdom and bless humanity. Most times, we cannot see the mind of Jesus, and instead of crying to God for the help of the Holy Spirit, we deceive people with false representation that negates what Jesus stands for. Our local assemblies have invented all kinds of activities and programs to replace the speakings of the

Lord. Just as we have described above, the Church ought not to seek her own or what pleases her but what pleases the Father through Jesus. When we cannot see and hear what God is doing or saying, we misguide the people by religious activities, human intelligence, and motivational speaking devoid of God's life.

The Church As A Place Of True Worship

> *"The time is coming, ma'am, when we will no longer be concerned about whether to worship the Father here or in Jerusalem. For it's not where we worship that counts, but how we worship–is our worship spiritual and real? Do we have the Holy Spirit's help? For God is Spirit, and we must have his help to worship as we should. The Father wants this kind of worship from us. But you Samaritans know so little about him, worshiping blindly, while we Jews know all about him, for salvation comes to the world through the Jews"* *(John 4:21-22, TLB).*

In the scripture above, Jesus again revealed a profound truth that may not have been understood until now. He shifted the hearts and minds of the people to a new paradigm from what they were used to. Before that statement, there were institutionalized places of worship, like Jerusalem, Mount Gerazim, Shiloh, and other places in the Bible.

Worshippers do go to those designated places for worship, or else God does not accept their worship. Hannah goes to Shiloh to worship. It means that it is only in those designated places of worship that the presence of God will be manifested to bring the needed help in their lives. Worshippers adore and reverence such places as the place of worship. The name of such places of worship in Israel is called Temple. The Jews have their temple in Jerusalem, separate from that of the Samaritans in mount Gerazim.

The difference in these places of worship is the social class that the woman confronted Jesus in John Chapter 4. She made a distinction between the Jews and the Samaritans. It was in the midst of that discussion that Jesus shifted her mind as He declared the new rule and said,

"Woman, believe me, the hour cometh when ye shall neither in this mountain nor yet at Jerusalem worship the Father.'

That statement automatically produced a change in the realm of the spirit."The implication is that true worship acceptable to the Father is no longer premised on physical buildings or locations such as Jerusalem or any of those places of worship aforementioned. Jesus raised the bar for the requirement of worshippers seeking true worship. For someone to now tell me to come to a place (a physical structure called temple) as the only place God will accept my worship (thanksgiving, prayers, offerings) is no longer correct. That person is still working in the old order.

Another striking point Jesus made during the discussion is that it is possible to worship what you do not know and assume you are worshiping what you know. My beloved, it is so sad to say that many people are worshipping what they do not know. They only do that because they see a multitude doing the same thing. There are many gods and other things people worship. Please don't be blindly led.

From Jesus' statement, the new place of worship is now a dimension called '**in spirit and in truth**.' If you intend to get the approval of your worship from the Father, it must be in this dimension. Please take a look at how a version (message) puts it in verse 23.

> "But the time is coming- it has, in fact, come when what you are called will not matter and where you go to worship will not matter. "*It is who you are and the way you live that counts before God.* Your worship must engage your spirit in the pursuit of truth. That's the kind of people the father is looking for."

From that statement, worship has changed from a physical place to a spiritual place where the Spirit of God dwells. It is now the believer's heart in connection with the Spirit of God in line with the inspired truth of God's word. So this becomes the environment through which true worship can breed before God irrespective of your geographical location. It doesn't matter whether you are in Jerusalem, Samaria, or any physical temple or any place of worship. The heart of a believer is a significant issue in the art of worship.

The next thing to look into is the meaning of worship.

Worship is beyond singing songs to God. It transcends into obedience. You can only worship someone you love, adore, and revere in high esteem. While making the ultimate sacrifice of his only son-Isaac to God, Abraham told his young men to wait while he and Isaac go up to worship. Gen 22:2-5

This is important because the Church that Jesus built should be the heart of true worship. Our lives as believers should default to total obedience and ultimate sacrifice.

The Church As A Place Of Glory

When we say the Body of Christ is the epitome of the glory of God on earth, we need first to understand what this glory means before being introduced to some relevant scriptures to this fact.

The oxford dictionary defines glory as fame, praise, honour that is given to somebody because he has achieved something significant. It means great beauty, special care for pride, respect, or pleasure.

Names synonymous with glory are; splendour, grandeur, majesty, magnificence. These names mean greatness, and whatever it is that deserves praise. It also means anything that is impeccable and faultless, of a very high standard and degree. It speaks of excellence. Glory cannot be hidden, no matter what. It is like a diamond that attracts attention irrespective of wherever it is.

The Body of Christ, the Church, is described as glorious, having these qualities mentioned above.

> *"Husbands love your wives, even as Christ also loved the church and gave himself for her that He might sanctify and cleanse her with the washing of the water by the word, that He might present her to himself a glorious church, not having spot or wrinkle or any such thing but that it should be holy and without blemish" (Ephesians 5:25-27).*

Paul, in this scripture, was describing the quality of life that needs to be in the Church before she is presented to her lover-the Lord Jesus Christ. God intends to manifest His glory on earth through His agent –the Church. The scripture we quoted above shows that the Church will not be raptured until she radiates the glory and splendor of God. The Church of Jesus Christ is not a bunch of weak people trying to make heaven or a collection of fearful people trying to leave this world because of the menace of the enemy. Instead, the Church should dispel the world's darkness because of the light of God in her. Believers should not be scared of the enemy; instead, the enemy is afraid of them. The following things declared in Ephesians 5:27 happen when the Church of Jesus Christ radiates in glory. She must acknowledge the Lordship of her master-the Lord Jesus

- She must be separated from the world (Babylon) and all its gripes.

- She must be ready to endure hardness and be prepared to go through severe pain to reveal the glory. Rom 8:17-18

- She must walk in unity. Once there is division and sectionalism, the glory will not radiate well.

What is the effect of a dying Church amid a hopeless world? The blind cannot lead the blind; instead, both will fall into a ditch. We see the Church today as blind, deaf, and stinking. No wonder the best of the world today run away from the Church. They feel the Church is meant for the poor, the unproductive, the weak, and the needy. The Church has taken the position of the beggar begging for alms, and when the world deeps a drop into our mouth out of our God's great resources, we jump up in appreciation and then go for thanksgiving. Oh! What a shame.

The Bible recorded that the Church will lend to nations but what we see today is the opposite; "Ichabod" the glory has departed. The Church should reign in excellence, purity, power, and beauty.

When Apostle Paul visited Athens, his presence caused the collapse of the majesty of the great goddess 'Diana.' There was a significant change in the atmosphere, not just in Ephesus, where this miracle took place but the whole of Asia in those days. That was a demonstration of the glory of the Kingdom of God. The Church in the days of the 'Acts of Apostles' was glorious. People who were not in the Church then were afraid to do something wrong because of the immense glory that would expose their secrets. It was this glory that revealed the lies and insincerity of Ananias and Sapphira. People could feel the power of God as they interacted with believers of those days.

The manifestation of this level of glory did not result from the various religious activity in local assemblies but their day-to-day lives. The Church was known and felt in every city they were. It has been said that the day the Church would leave the earth, Satan and his cohort would rejoice because there would be no more opposition to his devices.

In this end time, the real Church of Jesus Christ will rise in glory and splendor. Her fame would surpass any fame ever known. Great wisdom and excellence will be the hallmark of the Church as the Lord floods our hearts with His light and life in this end time. This glory will then radiate from us to the outside world.

> *"Rise up and shine, for your light has come. The shining-greatness of the Lord has risen upon you. For see, darkness will cover the earth. Much darkness will cover the people. But the Lord will rise upon you, and His shining-greatness will be seen upon you. 3 Nations will come to your light.*

And kings will see the shining-greatness of the Lord on you" (Isaiah 60:1-3, NLV).

The Church As A Spiritual Encampment

By encampment, we mean a spiritual location where people can find solutions, rest, and comfort in their troubles. The Church that Jesus built is intended to be an encampment for the battered, disposed of, abused, and troubled. It is a highly spiritual environment that allows the flow of angelic beings to assist as the needs arise. It is an environment paraded by heavenly angels on assignment, ascending and descending as seen in the dream when Jacob was going in search of a wife in Gen 28:12 the angels of God were present.

In this season, the Lord is increasing the level of angelic activities to minister to the Body of Christ as we move towards the end of the age.

The Church of Jesus Christ is not a club or social gathering for debates, nor is it a political party where member's selfish interest is uppermost in each heart but a spiritual environment that produces transformation inside out.

This spiritual encampment is the same as what God told Moses and Joshua to set up in the nation of Israel. They set up refuge cities and camps where people with specific problems can run to and find shelter and comfort.

"The Lord said to Joshua, tell the people of Israel to designate now the cities of refuge as instructed by Moses. If a man is guilty of killing someone unintentionally, he can run to one of those cities and be protected from the relatives of the dead man, who may try to kill him in revenge. When the innocent killer reaches any of the cities, he will meet the city council and explain what happened, and they must let him come in and give him a place to live among them. If a relative of the dead man comes to kill him in revenge, the innocent slayer must not be released to them, for the death was accidental" (Josh 20: 1-5).

The true Church of Jesus Christ acts as the refugee camps for the dispossessed, the blind, and wounded by the present system of false Christianity expressed in Josh 20: 1-5. The Church should be a resting place for leaders who are leaving the errors of the past and embracing the light of the present truth. The Church should be a place of rest, renewal, counsel, and advice to leaders who have good intentions and motives but mistakenly find themselves in the wrong environment. The Church is expected to provide life, truth, and redemption to individuals fleeing the darkness of the broken religious systems.

Note that when God talked to Moses in **Num 35:15**, the refugee camp is not meant for the Israelites alone but also for foreigners and travelers passing through their land. So the spiritual encampment is equally meant for those tired of occult entanglement due to false hope and expectation.

The Church must be strong enough to provide, protection, deliverance, and the pathway to find the true God and not the god of their belly.

> "*See, a king will reign in righteousness, and rulers will rule injustice. Each man will be like a shelter from the wind and a refuge from the storm, the streams of water in the desert, and the shadows of the great rocks in a thirsty land. Then the eyes of those who see will no longer be closed, and the ears of those who hear will listen. The mind of the rash will know and understand; the stammering tongue will be fluent and clear*" (Isaiah 32:1-4).

The scripture above is an accurate representation of the Church that will receive approval from God. The King and the rulers are the Lord Jesus with the leaders and the members of His church. This Church has to rule with righteousness and justice in all affairs she engages on earth. That is not all; the ultimate aim is to serve as shelter to lives when the strong demonic winds blow in the people's lives. We are to be a refuge for people amid storms; become a stream of water in the desert of life, become a great rock that cannot be crushed. Only when we do will the eyes of the blind be opened to our gospel, their ears will hear the good news, their dark mind will receive illumination. The eyes, ears, and hearts of nations, organizations, institutions, and individuals alike are itching to be opened so they can come into the reservoir of God's resources. Never in the history of humanity has this scripture been relevant as much as now.

The Lord is raising His Church to be a sanctuary (refuge city) on earth. Many have meddled with occultism and all manner of diabolical practices in the past and have been subjected to the fear of death. Now they are apprehensive that renouncing those practices would endanger their lives and their loved ones. As a result, they choose to remain in those practices even when it is evident that they are no longer enjoying them.

They want to see confidence and reassurance in this emerging Church that they will be protected just as the priests in those refugee cities ensure that the man-slayer is protected at all cost. It is not an easy task as the repercussions of that individual, nation, organization, or institution may come on you. However, when you succeed, you would have delivered a people, nation, etc., and verses 3 and 4 of the above scripture will be fulfilled.

This is the process by which the transfer of the nation's wealth into the Body of Christ will be accomplished. Why do you think the riches quoted in Isa 45:3 are deposited in the dark places? Today's material wealth is in the dark and secrets places (demon passed groups). Until we wade into the shelter of those structures and bring deliverance, we will not have access to those riches as God intended. The other way people can access it is by joining them, which is not the way of God.

There is a heart cry of nations, organizations, and individuals today for deliverance. Responding to these haet cries is far more than some pastors organizing a night prayer and laying hands on few individuals to cast out demons from them. The demons controlling territories, nations, systems, institutions are far more, and they eventually control the man you have delivered. God is calling us to broaden our minds about Him and His activities on earth.

The life of Job in **Job 29:1-17** is a typical lifestyle of any member of Jesus Body –the Church, so put yourself wherever the name of Job is mentioned:

"Job continued his discourse: how I long for the months gone by, for the days God watched over me when his lamp shone upon my head, and by his light, I walked through darkness! Oh, for the days when I was in my prime, when God's intimate friendship blessed my house and when the Almighty was still with me, and my children were around me when my path was drenched with cream, and the rock poured out for me streams of olive oil. When I went to the gate of the city and took my seat in the public square, the young men saw me and stepped aside, and the older men rose to their feet; the chieftain refrained from speaking and covered their mouths with their hand; the voices of the nobles were hushed, and their tongue stuck to the roof of their mouths. Whoever heard me spoke well of me, and those who saw me commended me <u>because I rescued the poor who cried for help and the fatherless who had none to assist him. The man who was dying blessed me; I made the widows' hearts sing. I put on righteousness as my clothing;</u>

justice was my robe and my turban. I was eyes to the blind and feet to the lame; I was a father to the needy; I took up the case of a stranger, I broke the fangs of the wicked and snatched the victims from their teeth."

The Church As A Place Of Strength And Power

The Church is regarded as a mighty fortress and a place of unassuming strength. In a book written by 'John Knox'- 'Give Me Scotland or I die,' it is said that the then Queen of England feared the power in the prayer of John Knox than the power of any armory of any nation in the world. There is enormous power in the prayer of a saint who is in proper alignment with God.

After the Lord Jesus had declared His church, He made a compelling statement affirming the strength and power that lies within her.

> *"And I will give you the keys of the kingdom of heaven and whatever you bind on earth will be bound in heaven and whatever you loose on earth will be loosed in heaven" (Matt 16:19).*

God gave the Church power of attorney to decide the fate of nations, organizations, and individuals. We have the keys to shaping things on earth according to the will of God. Unfortunately, the Church is failing in this responsibility. God did not give this power to one Senior Pastor or Bishop who intimidates the brethren. However, it is a collective responsibility to exercise that kingdom authority.

When brethren (kingdom believers), irrespective of their position in the church, agree on a particular thing, it will be done in heaven provided it is in line with God's will. Scripture says that the least in the Kingdom shall be like the men of David, as the angels of God.

> "On that day, the LORD will shield those who live in Jerusalem so that the feeblest among them will be like David, and the house of David will be like God, like the angel of the LORD going before them" (Zach 12:8).

You need to read the account of David and his men to grasp what this portion of the scripture is saying. To give a little clue to this, you can read 1Chronicles Chapters 11 and 12. As mighty as these men of David were, the Bible says that the least feeble in the Kingdom will do just what these great men did. That is the tremendous power residing in us. No wonder the scripture lamented that though 'we are gods but will die like mere men' because of not knowing who we are. The Church is expected to generate power and strength, but we run to the occult for power. This is sacrilege and an egregious error. What an insult! What a shame! What an anomaly!

In the world today, people fear the power of witchcraft than the believer's power. We profess God, quote all scriptures, and claim all promises in the Bible but have no corresponding power within us to activate what we are declaring. In the early Apostles' days, when the believers prayed, there was a physical shaking of the ground, and everyone was filled with the Holy Ghost.

"After they prayed, the place where they were meeting was shaken. And they were all filled with the Holy Spirit and spoke the word of God boldly" (Acts 4:31, NIV).

The Church of Jesus Christ must come back to this place of power and strength amid Babylon, so the world will know who our God is.

The Church As A Place Of Strong Governmental Prayers

"Then He taught, saying to them, "Is it not written, 'My house shall be called a house of prayer for all nations? But you have made it a 'den of thieves'" (Mark 11:17, NKJV).

"Therefore I exhort first of all that supplications, prayers, intercessions, and giving of thanks be made for all men, for kings and all who are in authority, that we may lead a quiet and peaceable life in all godliness and reverence, for this is good and acceptable in the sight of God our Saviour, who desires all men to be saved and to come to the knowledge of the truth" (1 Timothy 2:1-4).

The declaration of Jesus that "My house shall be called a house of prayer for all the nation" is emphasized' in all the gospel. This type of prayer is different from other forms of prayers the Church has been used to. It is called governmental prayer because it declares to the principalities and powers in the enemy's camp the heart of the apostolic impartation in the Church. It is a breakthrough and authoritative prayer, based on prophetic discernment of God's will, filled with prophetic utterances and apostolic decrees. It is the spoken word of God's power filling the earth.

This prayer is about asking (making demands) of God's will in the nations of the earth. It corroborates the pattern of prayer that Jesus taught us in the scripture.

> "Thy kingdom come; thy will be done in earth as it is in heaven" (Luke 11:2).

This prayer is governmental because it enforces the rulership and domain of God upon planet earth. It attacks the structures and systems of Babylon, which resists the supremacy of the Kingdom of God on earth. It is a prayer of the great demand for His will to be done on earth. Look at how THE MESSAGE version of the Bible puts this.

> "Let me tell you what God said next. He said, "You're my son, and today is your birthday. What do you want? Name it: Nations as a present? Continents as a prize? You can command them all to dance for you or throw them out with tomorrow's trash" (Psalm 2:7-9, THE MSG).

It is a prayer of decrees and proclamations of the judgment of God written says, Psalm 149:6-9. Through the power of prayer, the Kingdom of God and His rulership would come to the earth. There are forces in the atmosphere that continue to resist its manifestation. We need violent believers making violent declarations in prayer.

"And from the days of John the Baptist until the present time, the kingdom of heaven has endured violent assault, and violent men seize it by force (as a precious price- a share in the heavenly kingdom is sought with most ardent zeal and intense exertion" (Matt 11:12 AMP).

"… The kingdom of heaven has been forcefully advancing, and forceful man lay hold of it."

"The law and the prophet were proclaimed until John. Since that time, the good news of the kingdom of God is being preached, and everyone is forcing their way into it" (Luke 16:16, NIV).

I want to say that the only thing that matters to God now is establishing His Kingdom on earth. The Kingdom of God (the Kingdom of God is the same as the Kingdom of heaven) contains God's righteousness, lifestyle, operations, and everything a man needs to live with. This is beyond Church activities. It encompasses all the realms of God's creation and dominion.

There Are Two Areas Of Note

Firstly, this Kingdom is advancing in a forceful dimension against all the terrible satanic opposition set up to resist it. This Kingdom is a conquering force that cannot coexist peacefully with any kingdom with an opposing nature.

Secondly, of a necessity, this Kingdom needs the activities of men to advance its purpose on earth and make it real. The Kingdom is first birthed in the hearts of men before they forcefully and violently enforce it in all the nations of the world. These kingdom-advancing prayer people shake the spirit realm through strong governmental prayers.

In Acts Chapter 4, the Sadducees arrested Peter and John for preaching and healing the man at the Beautiful Gate. They severely threatened them not to preach the name and resurrection of Jesus. In response to their threat, the Church gathered and confronted the demonic threat calling down the power of the Holy Ghost. Their prayer shook the spirit realm to its foundations so much that it was physically felt in Jerusalem. That was a kingdom-advancing prayer. This is what we call governmental prayers.

God calls the Church today to be highly prophetic to see what He is saying in heaven and then declare it on earth. In this season, God is raising strong governmental prayer people to raise their voices against the structures of Babylon, declaring alternative government of God upon the earth.

> *"After these things, I saw another angel coming down from heaven, having great authority, and the earth was illuminated with his glory. And he cried mightily with a loud voice saying, "Babylon the great is fallen, is fallen and has become a dwelling place of demon…" (Rev. 18:1-2).*

Any church that is not working towards the return of Christ to reign on earth by declaring and establishing the Kingdom of God in all spheres of dominion is not working in order and therefore has missed the emphasis of the Spirit of God at this moment.

The Church As A Spiritual High Place

> "*The Lord God is my strength, and he will make my feet like hind's feet, and he will make me walk upon my high places. To the chief singer on my stringed instrument*" *(Habakkuk 3:19, NIV)*.

> "*He made me ride in the high places of the earth, that he might eat the increase of the fields; and he made him suck honey out of the rock, and oil out of the flinty rock*" *(Deuteronomy 32:13, NIV)*.

> "*Then shalt thou delight thyself in the Lord, and I will cause thee to ride upon the high places of the earth and feed thee with the heritage of Jacob, thy father; for the mouth of the Lord has spoken it*" *(Isaiah 58:14)*.

A high place is a spiritual location that controls the activities on earth. Every good or bad activity on the earth is hatched in high places. These high places are guarded by both angelic and demonic beings depending on whom you yield to. The high places work together with regulating the sun, the moon, the stars, and the heavenly bodies to invoke their intent on earth.

> "*Have you commanded the morning since your days began and caused the dawn to know its place, that it might take hold of the ends of the earth, and the wicked be shaken out of it? ...Can you bind the cluster of the Pleiades or loose the belt of Orion? Can you bring out Mazzaroth in its season? Or can you guide the great bear with its cubs? Do you know the ordinances of the heavens? Can you set their dominion over the earth?*" *(Job 38:12-13, 31-33, NKJV)*.

As potent and significant as these high places and heavenly bodies might be, humans manipulate them. They cannot initiate action without human instruction. The book of Job revealed that some people could break into the ordinances of heavenly bodies and enforce their dominion on earth.

As explained in the quoted scriptures at the beginning of this section, God has intended the Church to function in this realm of dominion. In any environment where the Church is located, it is expected to be the high place for the people in that environment. Through this means, God can further establish His will on the earth.

Evidently, we see the occult, the star-gazers, and diviners taking advantage of this opportunity given to the Church to profit the Kingdom of God, to cause mayhem against humanity. Sicknesses, diseases, and various kinds of viruses come through the air, so says the scientists, but many have not tried to find out how they come. Righteousness, breakthrough, and promotions also come through the same medium. Let's analyze this scripture below in light of the discussion at hand.

> "Blotting out the handwriting of ordinances that was against us, which was contrary to us, and took it out of the way, nailing it to the cross" (Colossians 2:14, NKJV).

The question here is who wrote the ordinance, and where was it written? It says the writings were contrary to us, which means it was not in line with the plan of God for our lives. The enemy wrote it in the high place which worked within the regulation of the sun and the moon; so year after year, generation after generation, the written curse keep working until someone of higher power than he that wrote it comes to cancel it.

I have met someone who says she always falls ill of a particular aliment in the month of August every year. That illness is not ordinary and defies every medical attention. Until the written ordinances are removed or deprogrammed in the high place, it reoccurs at the set time.

> *"Your enemies shall submit to you, and you shall tread down their high places"(Deuteronomy 33:29b).*

Both righteous and unrighteous sacrifices are performed at the altar, and altars are built in the high places of the earth (1Kgs 13:1-2; 1Sam 9:12; 1Chron 21: 26-29).

Decisions and discussions of kingship and rulership on the earth are made in the high place. 1Sam 9, 10. Samuel anointed Saul and even David in the high place. When great kings, rulers, presidents, governors, and business owners assume office or throne, they always try to take charge of the high places for their benefit.

There is always contention in the high places of the earth between light and darkness. Some nations represent the high places of the earth. These nations sometimes have more troubles than others, not necessarily because of their sins but their weight of responsibility. Nations that are high places always have other surrounding nations under them. Whoever controls the high places (either light or darkness) will affect their citizens and their operations and the activities of their neighboring nations.

The Church should grow up and ascend into the high realms in the spirit to deprogram the ancient program the enemy has written against the nations of the earth. On this ground, God was speaking to Jeremiah that He was setting him over the nations and kingdoms to root out, pull down, destroy, and throw down, build, and plant. He was meant to re-set activities in the high places over those nations. He was to root out, pull down, destroy, and throw down what the enemy has planted in the high places of those nations, and afterward, build and plant new things to advance God's Kingdom in those nations.

The founding fathers of the USA planted godliness, righteousness, good-living in their high places. That was the backbone that resulted in their greatness until recently when wickedness, immorality, and all manner of evil vices crept in and are now eating up their moral fabric—eroding their godly heritage as misguided fathers are now projecting evil things into their high places.

Living a righteous life is good but not enough to combat the menace of the evil one in high places. It cannot guarantee sustainable progress over time. King Asa was a good man who feared the Lord. He had a perfect heart unto the Lord but failed to remove the idols in the high places of his domain. Although God blessed him, he did not die well because of it. Read the following scriptures for further explanations: 2Chron 15, 16 (especially 15: 16, 17 & 16: 7-13); 1King 15:11-14.

There is a clarion call for the renewed Church to wake up to her spiritual responsibility of taking over the high places of the earth. Arise and be the voice David prophesied about in Psalm 24:7-10, a generation seeking the Lord and not their belly.

> *"Lift up your heads, O you gates! And be lifted up you everlasting doors! And the King of glory shall come in. Who is this King of glory? The Lord strong and mighty, the Lord mighty in battle. Lift up your heads, O you gates! Lift up, you everlasting doors! And the King of glory shall come in. Who is this King of glory? The Lord of hosts, He is the King of glory."*

Every nation, institution, organization, and individual has a gate, and the gatekeepers are very crucial to the life and activities of that nation, institution, or individual. They determine whether light or darkness comes to that nation. It is not just the policy or skill of the people that determine their success. These gatekeepers are highly spiritual, and their activities are done in high places.

King David, who also was a Prophet, understood these spiritual dynamics and raised a mighty declaration asking for a change of the gatekeepers of Israel so that the authentic King of glory could come in. This resulted in fierce spiritual contention. Understand that the previous gatekeepers will not surrender with ease. We have to relentlessly displace them because of our superior position of authority in Christ.

The Church As A Place Of Death To Self

> "*Most assuredly, I say unto you, unless a grain of wheat falls into the ground and dies, it remains alone; but if it dies, it produces much grains. He who loves his life will lose it, and he who hates his life in this world will keep it for eternal life" (John 12:24-25).*

> "*When he had called the people to himself, with his disciples also, he said to them, "Whoever desire to come after me, let him deny himself, and take up the cross and follow me. For whoever desires to save his life will lose it, but whoever loses his life for my sake and the gospel will save it" (Mk 8:34-35).*

Though Jesus was speaking to His disciples, invariable He was talking to the entire Church. He began describing the Church using a grain of wheat in John's gospel. So long as the seed is not planted in the ground and allowed to die, it will never grow up to bear fruit. That seed or grain of wheat which represents the Church must die. If not, she has no life in Christ. The next verse explained the manner of death God expects from the Church. You must hate yourself, take up your cross, then follow the Lord. Denying oneself is not a one-time event; it is a process the Church must be ready to go through as long as we are still on this earth. The only transition from man to God is through death.

Jesus Himself said that if there is no death, the seed (Church) abides alone. That death means you must deny yourself, take up your cross, and then follow. We have preached this message for a long time, but we have never understood the reality of what Jesus was saying. How do we deny ourselves? What is the cross? We cannot get the God kind of blessing and success that will last for eternity if we do not pass through this Death process.

> "... If indeed we suffer with him, we may also be glorified together with him. For I considered that the suffering of this present time are not worthy to be compared with the glory which shall be revealed in us" (Rom 8:17-18).

> "It is a faithful saying: for if we be dead with him, we shall also live with him; if we suffer, we shall reign with him; if we deny him, he will also deny us" (2Tim 2:11-12).

The Church wants to reign with Christ and enter into the glory of the Father, great! There is a price to pay, and the first price is that you must die to yourself. You cannot see God when you are still alive. This message cannot be overemphasised. All through the Bible, right from Genesis through Revelation, emphasis has been on humanity coming up to meet with his God, and the only way it can be expressed is through death. Jesus came to show us an example and paid the ultimate price, but daily, we ought to die to the affairs of this world as the Apostles admonished in the scripture.

> *"We must through many tribulations enter the kingdom of God" (Acts 14:22b:*

> *"Beloved do not think it straight concerning the fiery trial which is to try you, as though some strange things happened to you: but rejoice to the extent that you partake of Christ's sufferings that when His glory is revealed, you may also be glad with exceeding joy. If you are reproached for the name of Christ, blessed are you, for the spirit of glory and of God rests upon you" (1Peter 4:12-14).*

> *"I affirm, by the boasting in you which I have in Christ Jesus our Lord; I die daily" (1Cor 15:31).*

> *"My grace is sufficient for you, for My strength is made perfect in weakness. Therefore most gladly, I will rather boast in my infirmities that the power of Christ may rest upon me. Therefore I take pleasure in infirmities, reproaches, in needs, in persecutions, in distresses for Christ's sake. For when I am weak, then I am strong" (1Cor 12:9-10).*

As long as the Church remains a babe (not growing up into maturity), there won't be persecutions, trials, or dying to self. However, once she sets her heart to fulfill her obligations as mature sons of God, all of these sufferings and deaths will come. God takes delight when He sees His Church making the ultimate choice of leaving the world and its glory to come to Him.

The Church must go through three stages of this death process before we get to the holiest place where we can interface with God without any veil and show forth His unrestrained authority on earth.

Death To The Issues Of Our Body And The World Around Us

"Love not the world neither the things that are in the world. If any man loves the world, the love of the Father is not in him. For all that is in the world, the lust of the flesh, the lust of the eyes and the pride of life, is not of the Father, but of the world" (1John 2:15-16:).

"If then you were raised with Christ, seek then the things that are above where Christ is sitting at the right hand of God. Therefore put to death your members which are on the earth: fornication, uncleanness, passion, evil desire and covetousness which is idolatry" (Col 3:15).

"I beseech you therefore, brethren, by the mercies of God, that you present your bodies a living sacrifice, holy and acceptable to God which is your honourable service" (Rom 12:1).

The Bible says that being a friend of the world or loving the world is equivalent to being an enemy of God. This world here means the system and principles that govern the operations of this fallen and dark world. When we come to God, we receive a new appetite, and our taste buds change; our hearts shift from men's desire to God's desire. We carry a unique and enduring kingdom in our hearts to be birthed in the earth. We die to all of the world's desires, lust, and glamour that go with it. For every question the world asks us, we pull back to the Spirit of God to get an answer before responding. We are in this world, but we are not of this world. Our operating system is from heaven, which determines all the parameters of our lives. We die to every lust of the flesh and its carnal desires.

Death To Issue In Our Soulish Realm

"And do not be conformed to this world but be transformed by the renewing of your mind, that you may prove what that good and acceptable and perfect will of God" (Rom 12:2).

"Set your mind on things above, not on things on the earth. For you died, and your life is hidden with Christ in God. But now you yourselves are to put off all these: anger, wrath, malice, blasphemy, filthy language out of your mouth" (Col 3:2,3, 8).

We have to die to the issue of our minds. We can only get to God by the Spirit of God that resides in our human spirit. Our human knowledge can never please God except it becomes subject (death process) to God's Spirit. Through education, civilization, culture, and globalization, the world has given us an identity that is negative to God's identity in our lives. We must die to those identities of the world no matter how good they might look. We must die to our selfish ambitions, self-image, and self-esteem, achievements, or failures. We must die to all that we can get by ourselves.

Death To The Issues In Our Spirit Man

The purging must be entire if the Church is ready to meet with the Lord in the Most Holy place of God's tabernacle. No iota of sin is accommodated there. The Church must die to every spiritual disobedience. God wants to see nothing else in us apart from His Son. He wants the complete death of the man and the complete rise of His Son in us. That is the only thing that will suffice Him. The death process cannot be accomplished without the help of the Holy Spirit.

This dying is associated with sacrifice. The children of Israel coming to God for the atonement of sin will come with a bullock, and the priest will kill it and burn it on the altar before the Lord. The sacrifice must be killed, and the aroma goes to God as a sweet-smelling savor. He is not interested in our dying, but it's only through death that our love for Him is revealed. So He enjoys our dying to self. He wants a people He can be proud of and boast in the way He did concerning Job. He wants people that will show their unequivocal love to Him irrespective of their circumstance.

Someone once said,

"Sacrifice is the currency of transaction in eternity. It is the universal standard for converting our earthly endeavors to eternal value. A life stretched by sacrifice can never return to its original dimension."

Paul in Philippians 3: 1-14 described a way of achieving this death process in the life of every believer who wants to meet God. Verse 7-11 says,

"But what things were gained to me, these I have counted loss for Christ. Yet indeed I also count all things loss for the excellence of the knowledge of Christ Jesus my Lord, for whom I have suffered the loss of all things and count them as rubbish, that I may gain Christ and be found in Him, not having my own righteousness, which is from the law, but that which is through faith in Christ. This righteousness is from God by faith: that I may know him and the power of his resurrection and the fellowship of the sufferings, being conformed to His death, if by any means, I may attain to the resurrection from the dead."

Paul wants us to be conformed to Christ's death, to have a fellowship (partnership) in His sufferings, and after, experience the power of His resurrection.

To be conformed to His death means operating in the principles released and becoming alive when Christ died. We can refer to Christ's death as the "Cross." There are principles we can extract from Christ's death in Paul's message, which will be used when we die to the vices of the earth. There are thus:

Dying to self will dismantle the imperative of self and elevates the spirit of otherness, substitution, and representation. It will provide the correct filter through which we can view the outer world.

This dying to self will correct all the distortions of the past and the ravaging impact of the earthly life and time. It provides the portal to access divine authority, rank, and ascension.

The Church As A Place Of Continuous Growth And Increase

"For unto us a child is born, and unto us, a son is given, and the government will be upon his shoulder, and his name will be called Wonderful, Counselor, Mighty God, Everlasting Father, Prince of Peace. Of the increase of his government and peace, there will be no end upon the throne of David and over his Kingdom, to order it and establish it with judgement and justice from that time forward, even forever. The zeal of the Lord of host will perform this" (Isa 9: 6-7).

"But we all, with unveiled face, beholding as in a mirror the glory of the Lord, are being transformed into the same image from glory to glory, just as by the spirit of the Lord" (2 Corinthians 3:18).

"In whom the whole building, being fitted together, grows into a holy temple in the Lord" (Ephesians 2:21).

The Church of our Lord Jesus Christ is meant to be a place of divine growth and increase. There is no stagnation in the body. We are to grow in knowledge, wisdom, and revelation from our God. The Church is meant to be a repository center of divine resources to be dispatched to the earth. The scripture in Isaiah 9: 7 says that the increase of God's government on earth through his saints shall not end but shall be an everlasting one. It grows from glory to glory, from good to better and best.

The Church is a nation within Babylon that will teach Babylon the ways of God. Take a look at the life of Daniel in Babylon. He and his three friends, alongside others, were chosen by King Nebuchadnezzar to be trained to govern the affairs of Babylon. After the training, Daniel and his three friends were ten times better than others in their looks, character, intelligence, and all that the King requires. It was said about them that they had an excellent spirit from the gods.

God intends to govern the affairs of man on earth through His saint. The body of believers called the saints are to grow in all things, acquire skills and develop. This emerging Church is not a mediocre Church that cannot impact her environment. The impact of the Church on earth traverses all fields of human endeavors. It is not limited to the spiritual alone though it starts from there. That is who we are and where we came from (God). We are here on earth to showcase the multi-faceted dimensions of God's grace and wisdom in all of creation.

The Church of the Lord Jesus Christ is not and can never be stagnant. It is growing and forcefully advancing at every instance. The word of God can never be broken. The Church of Jesus Christ is moving forward, and the gates of hell cannot withstand it.

The individual members of this Church are expected to be different from the world and lead. The Church of Jesus is God's representatives on earth both in our conduct, our intelligence, and wisdom. We should be solving problems in our families, marriages, place of work, our environment, and wherever we find ourselves.

The list continues in our next edition.

Please watch out for it!

THE PURPOSE OF THE CHURCH ON EARTH

CHAPTER 5

THE CHURCH IN THE MIDST OF BABYLON

Reading this scripture in John Chapter 17 you will realise that it reveals one of the richest interactions and prayers of our Lord Jesus Christ to God, His Father about His Church before His imminent departure.

At the time of this prayer, the Lord Jesus was about leaving His disciples (The Church) in the world (Babylon) and returning to the Father in heaven. It was one of the most critical moments of His life and ministry on earth. He knew that His departure was at hand and was deeply concerned about leaving His Church in the world because of the voracious and evil nature of Babylon. At the same time, He was not asking the Father to take the Church away from the world because the Church has significant work to do on earth after His departure. Rather, He prayed that God should preserve her from the evil one

John 17

"Jesus spoke these words, lifted up His eyes to heaven, and said: "Father, the hour has come. Glorify Your Son, that Your Son also may glorify You, as You have given Him authority over all flesh, that He should give eternal life to as many as You have given Him. And this is eternal life, that they may know You, the only true God, and Jesus Christ whom You have sent. I have glorified You on the earth. I have finished the work which You have given Me to do. And now, O Father, glorify Me together with Yourself, with the glory which I had with You before the world was. "I have manifested Your name to the men whom You have given Me out of the world. They were Yours, You gave them to Me, and they have kept Your word. Now they have known that all things which You have given Me are from You. For I have given to them the words which You have given Me; and they have received them, and have known surely that I came forth from You; and they have believed that You sent

Me. "*I pray for them. I do not pray for the world but for those whom You have given Me, for they are Yours. And all Mine are Yours, and Yours are Mine, and I am glorified in them. Now I am no longer in the world, but these are in the world, and I come to You. Holy Father, keep through Your name those whom You have given Me, that they may be one as We are. While I was with them in the world, I kept them in Your name. Those whom You gave Me I have kept; and none of them is lost except the son of perdition, that the Scripture might be fulfilled. But now I come to You, and these things I speak in the world, that they may have My joy fulfilled in themselves. I have given them Your word; and the world has hated them because they are not of the world, just as I am not of the world. I do not pray that You should take them out of the world, but that You should keep them from the evil one. They are not of the world, just as I am not of the world. Sanctify them by Your truth. Your word is truth. As You sent Me into the world, I also have sent them into the world. And for their sakes I sanctify Myself, that they also may be sanctified by the truth. "I do not pray for these alone, but also for those who will believe in Me through their word; that they all may be one, as You, Father, are in Me, and I in You; that they also may be one in Us, that the world may believe that You sent Me. And the glory which You gave Me I have given them, that they may be one just as We are one: I in them, and You in Me; that they may be made perfect in one, and that the world may know that You have sent Me, and have loved them as You have loved Me. "Father, I desire that they also whom You gave Me may be with Me where I am, that they may behold My glory which You have given Me; for You loved Me before the foundation of the world. O righteous Father! The world has not known You, but I have known You; and these have known that You sent Me. And I have declared*

to them Your name, and will declare it, that the love with
which You loved Me may be in them, and I in them."

The tone of Jesus' voice in that prayer reveals that if it were possible for Him, He would have taken the Church along. But because He knew that the Church has a crucial task to accomplish on earth, He only prayed that the Father should preserve them in the world through His name. He also prayed that they should be united as one just as they (trinity) are one. It is only through their unity that they can execute God's purpose on the earth.

"Until we all reach unity in the faith and in the knowledge
of the Son of God and become mature, attaining to the
whole measure of the fullness of Christ" (Ephesians 4:13).

Babylon is a system that seductively entangles the Church into the web of immorality, uncleanness, disobedience to God and His principles, and all kinds of wicked vices that are against God's way of life. The Babylonian system creates a pseudo-god in people's lives, making them believe they are serving God, but indeed, they are serving mammon.

"But mark this: There will be terrible times in the last days.
People will be lovers of themselves, lovers of money, boastful,
proud, abusive, disobedient to their parents, ungrateful,
unholy, without love, unforgiving, slanderous, without
self-control, brutal, not lovers of the good, treacherous,
rash, conceited, lovers of pleasure rather than lovers of God,

having a form of godliness but denying its power. Have nothing to do with such people" (2 Tim 3:1–5, NIV).

We are in the world, but we are not of the world. Babylon should not have any hold on us. Though we are to interface with Babylon, we are meant to come out clean, just like Daniel and his three friends. The intent of Babylon is always to subvert the purpose of God and defile the Church.

> *"Now many nations are assembled against you, saying, "Let her be defiled, and let our eyes gaze upon Zion." But they do not know the thoughts of the LORD; they do not understand his plan, that he has gathered them as sheaves to the threshing floor. Arise and thresh, O daughter of Zion, for I will make your horn iron, and I will make your hoofs bronze; you shall beat in pieces many peoples; and shall devote their gain to the LORD, their wealth to the Lord of the whole earth" (Micah 4:11–13, ESV).*

God's purpose is to establish His kingdom on planet earth through His Church. He wants to rule over the nations of the world through His Church. Considering the current events across the globe today, it seems like an illusion for it to happen. The rising of the Islamic extremists trying to topple the government of nations, insecurities, and kidnappings in several places of the earth, immorality in the highest order (gay marriages, lesbianism, incest, pornography, and indecent dressing and music taking over our media), corruption and all evil vices are taking the uppermost in the lives of people. Moral decadence and corruption in private and public sectors are on the rise in unprecedented manners.

More concerning is the emergence of fake and unlearned so-called 'ministers of God' who retard the people of God instead of advancing them towards God and His purpose. With all these happening, people who are clueless about God's supremacy might think God and His people cannot take over the rulership of the earth before the evil day comes. However, that is a lie of the devil. The word of God stands sure. God cannot speak and fails to perform it. He is the creator and controller of the universe.

Listen To His Words:

> *"For truly I tell you, until heaven and earth disappear, not the smallest letter, not the least stroke of a pen, will by any means disappear from the Law until everything is accomplished"* (Matt 5:18, NIV).

> *"Heaven and earth [as now known] will pass away, but My words will not pass away"* (Matt 24:35, AMP).

> *"Yet it is easier for heaven and earth to pass away than for a single stroke of a letter of the Law to fail and become void"* (Luke 16:17, AMP).

> *"So will My word be which goes out of My mouth; It will not return to Me void (useless, without result), Without accomplishing what I desire, And without succeeding in the matter for which I sent it"* (Isa 55:11, AMP).

"The grass withers, the flower fades, But the word of our God stands forever" (Isa 40:8, AMP).

The scriptures above explain the authenticity, validity, and trustworthiness of God's word. The Lord says He has exalted His word above His name.

"I will bow down toward your holy temple and will praise your name for your unfailing love and your faithfulness, for you have so exalted your solemn decree that it surpasses your fame"(Ps 138:2, NIV).

His words are words of an oracle, and they are sure and absolute. Our God does not speak carelessly.

"For the word of God is alive and powerful. It is sharper than the sharpest two-edged sword, cutting between soul and spirit, between joint and marrow. It exposes our innermost thoughts and desires" (Heb 4:12).

In the early chapters of this book, we talked about God's purpose over the earth and gave some scriptural references explaining the desire of God to take over the earth and fill it with the knowledge of His glory.

"But [the time is coming when] the earth shall be filled With the knowledge of the glory of the Lord, As the waters cover the sea" (Hab 2:14, AMP).

The following scriptures are references to buttress God's original intent to fill the entire planet earth with His glory.

Prayerfully read through them all, and may the Lord grant you understanding in all things.

Isa 6:3; Ps 57:5; Ps 72:19; Num 14:21; Ps 57:11; 108: 4-5; Matt 6:10; Isa 2:11; 37:20; 11:9.

Jesus already said it when He instituted His Church that the kingdom of darkness will try to prevail (they will fight so hard and relentlessly that many might even think they are winning). However, suddenly, the Church will prevail because the gates of hell cannot overrun her.

Romans 9:28 says,

> *"For He will finish the work and cut it short in righteousness, because the LORD will make a short work upon the earth."*

And how will this be? The answer is here.

> *"Behold, the days are coming," says the LORD, "When the plowman shall overtake the one who gathers the harvest, and the one who treads the grapes [shall overtake] him who sows the seed [for the harvest continues until planting time]; When the mountains will drip sweet wine. And all the hills shall melt [that is, everything that was once barren will overflow with streams of blessing" (Amos 9:13, AMP).*

> *The time will come," says the LORD, "when the grain and grapes will grow faster than they can be harvested. Then the terraced vineyards on the hills of Israel will drip with sweet wine! (Amos 9:13, NLT).*

The Lord will cause a quick maturity of believers in this end time to bring in the harvest. A prophetic and apostolic people that will discern the will of the Lord and receive the grace to execute it without any fear or favor. A people that will not be corrupted by the religious systems of our day. A people whose heart and desire are fixed to do the will of the Father. A people that will not be defiled by the delicacies of the kings (the pastors, the bishops, and all the merchandising going on in the Church).

There is a war between light and darkness, righteousness and unrighteousness, and the kingdom of God and the kingdom of the devil. This war is a divine call to enforce the eternal victory secured by the Lord Jesus Christ over Satan and his kingdom of darkness. God is raising sons that will fight on His behalf and set the captives free from the clutches of hell. (A father fights for his children, but a son fights on behalf of his Father, having been trained by him. A child is always asking for help and making demands from his Father, while a son takes responsibility to protect his Father's estate. Even nature teaches us these things.

The question here is, who are you? A child or a son? This is the distinguishing factor in the things of the spirit. Unfortunately, so many who claim to be sons are children because of their attitudes to God and the things of God.

Surprisingly, not every member of the Church will be part of this company of sons. But that does not mean that if you are not there, you are no longer a member of God's people, no. It only means that you are not part of the remnant. You are not part of the Church within the Church. You are not part of the first fruits that will taste the powers of the world to come. You are not part of the army of the Lord that will salvage the others from calamity and desolations of this age. You are not part of the people the Lord will depend on to fight and enforce His kingdom, His truth, and guide His people navigate through conflicting desires and interests that confront us daily. You are not part of the army of believers that will forcefully advance the kingdom on earth, as we await His glorious return.

Certainly, it is only fully grown and matured sons that God can commit His burdens concerning the earth to. That son must have developed capacity over time in the area God is giving him responsibility. He must be a son who is or has a great interest in migrating from the outer court to the innermost court of our God.

The House Of The Lord

There are three significant compartments in the tabernacle of the Lord:

- The outer court

- The inner court (The Holy Place)

- The inner most court (The Holy of Holies)

As sons in His house, God intends to transition us from the outer court until we get to the holy of holies. The tabernacle of the Lord is a complete expression of a believer's walk and the Church, from the beginning (salvation) till the end of the journey (God). The first experience is that the house has a wide gate. This gate represents our Lord Jesus Christ, who alone is the way to God.

The Outer Court

When you come in through the gate by the conviction of the Hoy Spirit, you will get to the outer court. There are two objects in the outer court.

The First Object Is The Brazen Altar: This is where the animals are killed and sacrificed to the Lord. It is the first experience of a believer on his journey to God. Jesus represents the animal being killed. He receives the forgiveness of sin and the assurance of salvation on our behalf.

The Second Object Is The Laver: The laver was a bowl made of bronze to hold water for priests in ceremonial cleansing. The priest (the believer) must dip himself into that water for cleansing before going into the holy place for worship and service unto the Lord. In this outer court, you have a lot of Levites here to perform this sacrifice. This means every believer is here irrespective of who you are, provided the blood of Jesus has washed your sins. Some believers and even ministries build their lives in this outer court, constantly preaching repentance and forgiveness of sins. Though, it is needful to preach and revisit the message of repentance, but the truth is that God desires that we move on to the next level of maturity while still walking in the knowledge of this experience.

The Inner Court (The Holy Place)

The next compartment is the inner court (the holy place). You first notice that only priests are allowed here (priests are a particular set of Levites). Not all Levites are permitted here. This compartment represents a higher capacity compared to the previous compartment-the outer court. At this stage the believer is beginning to build a relationship with God. He now knows his purpose in life and what he is called to do on earth. He currently realizes his new creation realities and his identity in Christ, etc. There are three objects or experiences in this inner court.

1. The table of shewbread

2. The altar of incense

3. The golden lampstand

The First One Is The Table Of Shewbread: It talks about the bread in the house of the Lord, which represents the word of the Lord. The twelve loaves represent each tribe in Israel.

It means there is enough food for all the members of the Body of Christ. This talks about understanding the word of God, thereby building precept upon precept, line upon line, and knowing the promises of God in His word. Coming to the place of the logos of God, some believers and even some ministries encamp around this experience for too long.

The Second One Is The Altar Of Incense: It talks about where the priest stands before God with the sweet fragrance of the incense to offer up to God. This has to do with prayers. Some believers grow in the place of prayers. You have people who develop this into prayer ministry, deliverance ministry, watchmen, etc. This is good but not the finality of God. He wants us to move forward still.

The Third One Is The Golden Lampstand: Here, the priest ministers to the Lord from the holy place with the light from the candlesticks of this golden lampstand. This represents revelation, gifts of the Spirit, and manifestations of the Spirit. As I said before, some believers and ministries equally camp around this as their all in God. But God is saying that we must move if we must see God and be the REMNANT that will bear the burdens of the Lord over the nations.

The Most Inner Court (Holy Of Holies)

At the Holy of Holies, there is no more veil demarcating the holy place and the holy of holies in the new creation reality. After Jesus was sacrificed on the cross, the veil was torn from top to bottom, and the blood of Jesus granted us unlimited access into the Holy of Holies, the very presence of God. Every believer has the same access to the holy of holies. But the first thing to notice in this third and final compartment of the house of the Lord is that fewer priests function here. Only the high priest can serve here, thus indicating that higher capacity is required to operate here. Now every believer can operate here and potentially have the capacity to do so. You cannot function in the holy of holies with the same capacity you functioned within the holy place.

These capacities in the three compartments are not measured only on your spirituality level. It is equally measured on the degree of the assignment given to you by God. In this place, the priest's function is mainly for the people, which means your responsibility at this level is for the people, nations, organizations, and less about yourself.

The holy of holies is where God dwells. It is filled with a thick and powerful presence called the shekinah glory of God. The only piece of furniture there is the Ark of Covenant that contains three essential things.

The first content in the Ark of Covenant is the Ten Commandments, which symbolize God's government. The first five speaks of our relationship with God, while the other five speaks of our relationship with man. This dimension is where God puts His burden upon the believer, who is matured in God and skillful in the things of God. At this point, God begins to partner with the believer and ministries in creating a new government, initiating new policies and constitutions on how lives can be lived, co-partnering with the Lord in bringing both blessings and divine judgments upon the earth.

Isa 26:9b-10 says, When your judgments come upon the earth, the people of the world learn righteousness. But when grace is shown to the wicked, they do not learn righteousness; even in a land of uprightness, they go on doing evil and do not regard the majesty of the LORD.

The second content in the Ark of Covenant is The Golden Bowl of Manna, which symbolizes God's providence. This is the supernatural providence to feed and to bless the nations. It includes the supernatural ability to stop evil over the lives of people and nations.

The third content of the Ark of Covenant is Aaron's Rod that budded. This speaks of the magnificent power of God over His people. It is the power of God over the nations. The nations will fear God and His people because of the greatness of His power.

Psalms 66:3 says,

> *"How awesome are your works! Through the greatness of Your power, your enemies shall submit themselves to You."*

It takes the demonstration of the incredible power of the Lord by the Kingdom believers for the enemies of God to submit themselves.

One thing I know for sure is that before the Church leaves this earth, she will display some extraordinary manifestation of God's power that will terrify the kingdom of darkness and make them shiver to their bones.

God has always wanted to incubate man to produce sons of God on earth to fulfill the mandate in Genesis 1:26-28.

> "Then God said, "Let us make mankind in our image, in our likeness, so that they may rule over the fish in the sea and the birds in the sky, over the livestock and all the wild animals,[a] and over all the creatures that move along the ground." So God created mankind in his own image, in the image of God he created them; male and female he created them. God blessed them and said to them, "Be fruitful and increase in number; fill the earth and subdue it. Rule over the fish in the sea and the birds in the sky and over every living creature that moves on the ground."

These sons will possess the character and DNA of God. This is what will enable the Church to fulfill her purpose on earth before the return of the King and the establishment of His eternal Kingdom on earth.

> "Jesus Gave Them This Answer: Very truly I tell you, the Son can do nothing by himself; he can do only what he sees his Father doing, because whatever the Father does the Son also does. For the Father loves the Son and shows him all he does. Yes, and he will show him even greater

works than these, so that you will be amazed. For just as the Father raises the dead and gives them life, even so the Son gives life to whom he is pleased to give it. Moreover, the Father judges no one, but has entrusted all judgment to the Son, that all may honor the Son just as they honor the Father. Whoever does not honor the Son does not honor the Father, who sent him. "Very truly I tell you, whoever hears my word and believes him who sent me has eternal life and will not be judged but has crossed over from death to life. Very truly I tell you, a time is coming and has now come when the dead will hear the voice of the Son of God and those who hear will live. For as the Father has life in himself, so he has granted the Son also to have life in himself. And he has given him authority to judge because he is the Son of Man. "Do not be amazed at this, for a time is coming when all who are in their graves will hear his voice and come out—those who have done what is good will rise to live, and those who have done what is evil will rise to be condemned. By myself I can do nothing; I judge only as I hear, and my judgment is just, for I seek not to please myself but him who sent me" (John 5:19-30).

Testimonies About Jesus

"If I testify about myself, my testimony is not true. There is another who testifies in my favor, and I know that his testimony about me is true. "You have sent to John and he has testified to the truth. Not that I accept human testimony; but I mention it that you may be saved. John was a lamp that burned and gave light, and you chose for a time to enjoy his light. "I have testimony weightier than that of John. For the works that the Father has given me to finish—the very works that I am doing—testify that the Father has sent me. And the Father who sent me has

himself testified concerning me. You have never heard his voice nor seen his form, nor does his word dwell in you, for you do not believe the one he sent. You study ˢ the Scriptures diligently because you think that in them you have eternal life. These are the very Scriptures that testify about me, yet you refuse to come to me to have life. "I do not accept glory from human beings, but I know you. I know that you do not have the love of God in your hearts. I have come in my Father's name, and you do not accept me; but if someone else comes in his own name, you will accept him. How can you believe since you accept glory from one another but do not seek the glory that comes from the only God? "But do not think I will accuse you before the Father. Your accuser is Moses, on whom your hopes are set. If you believed Moses, you would believe me, for he wrote about me. But since you do not believe what he wrote, how are you going to believe what I say?" (John 5:31-47).

Other Book Authored By

TONY AZONUCHE

Tony is a skillful and a prolific writer, and a business strategist with vast experience in the subject matters of the Gospel of the Kingdom and the King and His Kingdom. He is a Dynamic

Minister of the Lord Jesus Christ, with an unflinching passion to see the full manifestation of the Kingdom of God here on earth.

Tony is the Convener of the Joshua Generation Movement, a Kingdom-based organization poised to execute the mandate of God: *"Thy kingdom come, thy will be done on earth as it is done in heaven.*

PRINCIPLES FOR BUILDING IN THE KINGDOM

In this book; the author elucidated with examples that life on earth is regarded as a building, and God has ordained principles and patterns that every building should follow to receive His approval.

Find out those patterns and principles and how to apply them to your daily life, as you sojourn here on earth.

Get copies for yourself, friends and families.

It is a must read for every Kingdom-minded believer.

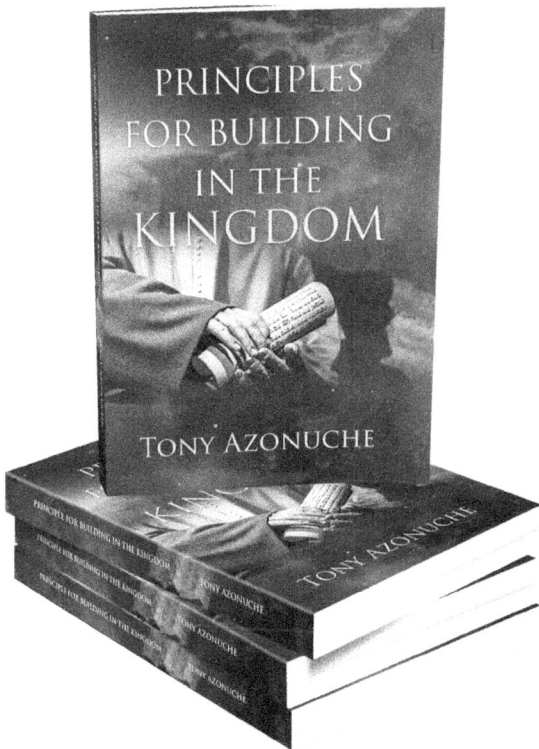

HOW TO GET COPIES OF HIS BOOKS

You can order copies Online on **www.amazon.com**

OR

Author's Direct Contact
Tony Azonuche
tonyazonuche@gmail.com
Tel: 1 (832) 419-7961, (832) 419-7988
Convener: Joshua Generation Movement.
joshuagenmovt@gmail.com

For Teachings, Seminars, Workshops on Kingdom Dimensions.

Reflection Point

Personal Notes: _____

_____

_____

_____

_____

_____

_____

_____

_____

=========== *Guided Action Plan* ===========

_____

_____

_____

_____

_____

_____

_____

Reflection Point

Reflection Point

Personal Notes: ———————————————————————————

_____

_____

_____

_____

_____

_____

_____

_____

_____

====================== *Guided Action Plan* ======================

_____

_____

_____

_____

_____

_____